# SEXUAL BLOOPERS

An outrageous, uncensored collection of people's most embarrassing x-rated fumbles!

## COMPILED AND ILLUSTRATED BY MICHELLE HORWITZ

A Fireside Book
Published by Simon & Schuster
New York     London     Toronto     Sydney     Singapore

FIRESIDE
Rockefeller Center
1230 Avenue of the Americas
New York, NY 10020

For information regarding special discounts for bulk purchases,
please contact Simon & Schuster Special Sales at
1-800-456-6798 or business@simonandschuster.com

FIRESIDE and colophon are registered trademarks of Simon & Schuster, Inc.

Designed by Diane Hobbing of Snap-Haus Graphics

Library of Congress Cataloging-in-Publication Data

Sexual bloopers : an outrageous, uncensored collection of people's most embarrassing x-rated
fumbles! / compiled and illustrated by Michelle Horwitz.
p.    cm.
"A Fireside book"
ISBN 0-7432-2695-X
1. Sex—Humor.    I. Horwitz, Michelle.

PN6231.S54 S42 2003
306.7'02'07—dc21                    2002042774

Manufactured in the United States of America

10   9   8   7   6   5   4   3   2   1

## *ACKNOWLEDGMENTS*

I absolutely *must* thank all those wonderfully courageous people out there who managed to overcome their initial reluctance and admit the truth! Without their outrageously candid confessions, and permission to go on record with their most embarrassing bloopers, I would only have had my own (not that *mine* couldn't have filled a book)!

A very special thanks goes to my hip, colorful, and brilliant editor Cherise Grant, who got it, and loved my idea immediately, then enthusiastically toiled with me to make it even better. Because of her, my first time "making book" was an amazing and unforgettable experience!

And finally, I'm forever grateful to the writer Colette for the timeless inspiration of her words: "You will do foolish things, but do them with enthusiasm!"

## *DEDICATION*

For Sherry, my patient and devoted listener through all those long talks and *very* long talks! Thank you for the reassuring fold of your arms that continually reminds me of your unshakeable faith in my dreams. For the last twenty-five years, everything of meaning has been framed in our love and every generous gift of your heart has been treasured by mine.

# CONTENTS

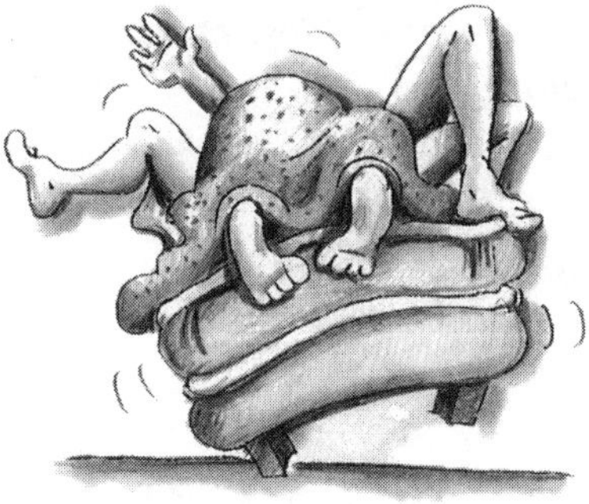



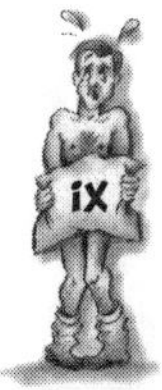

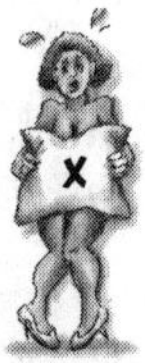
X

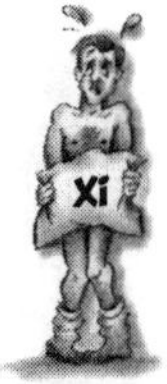
xi

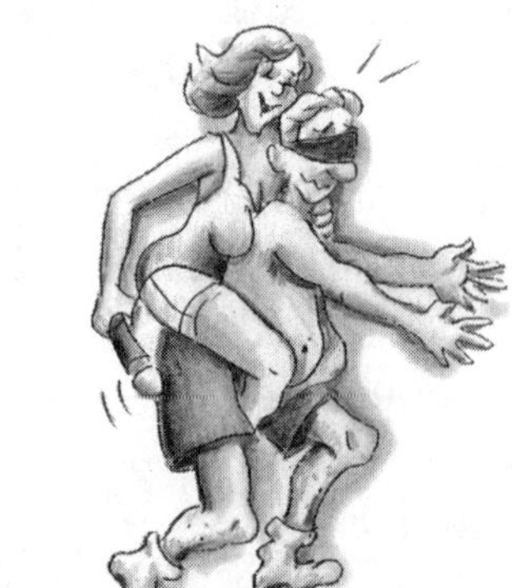

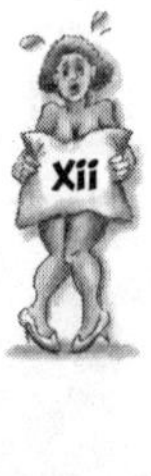
Xii

## FOREPLAY

It was on a lazy afternoon, lost in easy conversation with a close and trusted friend, that I somehow found myself divulging some rather embarrassing sexual details—traumatic things I had never, *ever* told anyone before! Greatly amused and inspired by my honesty, she in turn began confessing to some of her own. It was there on my living room floor, with both of us consumed in hysterical laughter (and admitted relief) that the idea for *Sexual Bloopers* was born!

Let's face it: Sex means *more* things to *more* people than probably any other human experience. Not surprisingly then, it manages to subject us to a fair amount of grief along with those moments of pleasure and glory. From the moment we first discover our genitals to the time we can no longer find them, we are either living in exhaustive pursuit of our sexual fantasies or lamenting the improbability of ever actually experiencing them. To make matters worse, we are continually bombarded by media hype deliberately and mercilessly aimed at our collective insecurities and vulnerable libidos. DEVELOP THE WORLD'S SEXIEST BODY! BECOME THE WORLD'S GREATEST LOVER! HAVE THE WORLD'S HOTTEST SEX! The message is that anything *else* is totally unacceptable and unspeakable!

Bookstores are chockful of stuff on sex, but consider the existing choices. Countless rows of romance novels packed with steamy and erotically charged scenarios tell us how our sex lives *should* be if only we lived in a fantasy world of bulging crotches and voluptuous bosoms all aching to be set free. Another aisle offers us an endless selection of visually enticing how-to manuals that glorify everything from ancient lovemaking potions and practices to every conceivable sexual position known to mankind. Each page explicitly depicts how

over-the-top our sex lives *could* be if only we were all Gods and Goddesses amorous and adventurous enough to harness the awesome potential of our own sexuality.

Offered up in refreshing contrast to these unrealistic quest-driven venues, *Sexual Bloopers* relies solely on the liberating honesty of real-life confessions. Under *this* cover, readers of all ages and sexual persuasions will finally find a much more honest account of it all—a blushing, uninhibited, and hilarious peek *behind* the scenes at what our sexual experiences are *really* like when we dare to tell the truth!

In the course of eliciting such highly personal anecdotes from others, what became immediately apparent was that truth-telling turned out to be as instantly disarming as it was contagious. Once people got over their initial and understandable reluctance to tell all, one confession led to another and another and another! Word of my project spread, and before long I was getting unsolicited calls and mail from people who knew people, each hoping I would include *their* blooper in the collection as well. Colorful and explicit, the confessions came from men and women, young and old, gay, straight, and every lifestyle in between. They divulged stories on everything from masturbation to experimental sex, first-times to fetishes, sex toys gone dead to seductions gone miserably wrong! Refreshingly candid and outrageously revealing, these anecdotes finally expose the naked truth about our *less* than perfect bodies often having *less* than rock-your-world sex! They are an open, honest, joyful admission of our many misconceptions, inadequacies and x-rated fiascos from even *before* the time we grow pubic hair until way *past* the time it begins to gray and thin out.

With everything from "educational" tapes to sidewalk sleaze promoting all the ways our sex lives can be *better, hotter,* and *wilder, Sexual Bloopers* finally offers the erotic-weary masses the relief we secretly crave and deserve. One confession after another reassures us that contrary to what all those writhing, throbbing media images would have us believe, it is *not* the ones with the longest penises or the largest breasts, but rather those of us endowed with a healthy sense of humor about it all, who *really* get to enjoy our sexuality the most.

I'm hopeful that *Sexual Bloopers,* in its liberating honesty, lets us all cum together in one great *comic*—if not always *orgasmic*—sigh of uninhibited release!

# CHAPTER I

# THE BIRDS AND THE BEES

## TALES FROM PUBERTY AND THE AGE OF INNOCENCE

# A CAN IN THE HAND IS WORTH TWO IN THE BUSH
## Carla, 47

I couldn't have been more than 10 when a new deodorant product, F.D.S., came on the market. Hoping to get women to try it, the manufacturer gave out samples in the store. My mother took one home and placed it in our medicine cabinet, right next to the aerosol can of Arrid. My older sister was 14; I noticed *she* had begun using deodorant spray under *her* arms, just like our mom did. Wanting desperately to be grown up like them, *I* secretly started using it, too. Underneath the large letters, FDS, were the words *feminine deodorant spray*. I hadn't the *slightest* idea what that meant. As far as I could tell, it was just another brand of deodorant.

One day, my mother happened to catch me spraying the FDS under my arms. Taking the can from my hand and replacing it with the Arrid, she smiled and explained that the FDS was a special kind of deodorant, not meant for underarms. I looked at her, completely puzzled. "Where *do* you use it, then?" I asked. Her answer was very straightforward: "It's for a woman to spray on her pubic hair to keep it smelling fresh." I looked at her like she was out of her mind! "Eeeuuu!" I said as I strained to grasp her explanation. "Who smells you down *there?*"

To this day, I get a private little chuckle every time my husband of 25 years goes down on me.

Once again I found myself standing behind the line on the class-room floor trying to read the eye chart.

## *20 / 20 HINDSIGHT*
*Wayne, 50*

Though I'd like to think of myself as much more sexually savvy today, I can never forget my very humble (and shortsighted) beginnings.

I had a very strict Catholic upbringing. Sex—or anything remotely connected to it—was *never, ever* discussed in the light of day. In spite of this (or maybe *because* of it), I was all of 10 when I discovered the secret thrill of jacking myself off. Despite the fact that I'd heard some really scary things could happen to a kid as a result of such sinful behavior (like going blind), I still went at it pretty regularly for the next few months. For a while there, I thought I was actually able to sneak one past God . . . until the results of my school eye test indicated that I now needed reading glasses. God had seemingly discovered my dirty little secret! Fearing his wrath, I made an earnest attempt to stop and repent, but I just couldn't seem to give it up permanently, and within a few short weeks, I was back to my old tricks. Another school year went by and, once again, I found myself standing behind the line on the classroom floor, trying to read the eye chart that hung from the blackboard. Much to my horror, my vision had gotten even *worse* and a stronger pair of glasses was now required! Now I was *really* getting worried, especially since I saw no end in sight for my evil ways. I started taking note of other kids and grown-ups who wore glasses and assumed they too were secretly taking their chances and jacking off just like me. Sometimes, I'd ask to look through other people's glasses. If their lenses were stronger than mine I'd feel a bit relieved, believing I still had a way to go before I lost my sight entirely!

By the time I was on my third prescription, I was seriously depressed. Living with my terrible secret was taking its toll. By now, I was sure I was going blind, and equally sure I could never stop masturbating.

One day, my 16-year-old brother caught me walking around my room with a blindfold on. When he asked me what I was doing, I admitted that I was practicing for when I went completely blind.

"Why in the world do you think you're going to go blind?" he asked.

I was really reluctant to tell him the truth . . . especially since *he* didn't wear glasses. But my heart was so heavy I had to confide in *someone,* so I confessed the whole thing to him. He practically peed in his pants laughing and assured me that except for the word *eyeball,* the two had *absolutely nothing* to do with each other!

Years later, after I graduated from college, I took a job with an organization that trained dogs for various handicapped people—among them, the blind. I called my brother and told him about the work I was doing. There was a long silence—then he burst out laughing and said, "Still worried, huh, kid?"

# A DOWN-AND-DIRTY MOTHER'S DAY
## Gary, 35

Back in the early '70s, when I was about six, my folks bought a house and moved my 13-year-old twin sisters and me out to the suburbs. We were one of the first families to move to the block, so there was still lots of construction going on around us. All this activity only added to my evergrowing boyhood obsession with toy trucks and construction vehicles of all kinds. I spent hours playing in the dirt, mimicking the activities of the crew breaking ground in the lot across the street. I had a dumpster, a forklift, a pickup, and a bulldozer . . . all with moveable parts! My dad even showed me how to make a working crane out of my erector set. The tall crane was my favorite. I loved how it could move huge amounts of earth from one place to another! One morning, I happened to be passing my parents' room and overheard my mother talking to my dad from behind their closed door. "Last night was incredible," she said, "I actually felt the earth move!" I was confused. I was in the house last night, too, but I didn't feel a thing! Besides, I always thought the workmen went home to their families at night and came back in the morning. When I repeated what I'd heard to one of my sisters, she made fun of me. "That's what's *supposed* to happen when two people have sex," she said. I didn't dare admit I had absolutely no idea what the hell *sex* was! In my little boy's mind, I figured that since it had to do with moving the earth, it must have meant playing in the dirt with toy trucks. I was surprised but happy to learn that this activity seemed to thrill my mother as much as it did me. So, when Mother's Day approached just a few weeks later, I knew exactly how I'd make her happy.

That morning, we all gathered around as mom read her cards and cried. "Before I open my presents, let's call grandma and wish *her* a happy Mother's Day, too" she said. We all agreed that would be a nice idea and, one by one, each of us got on the phone to talk to her. As usual, my chatty sisters went first, and stayed on practically forever. By the time they passed me the phone, I could hardly wait to tell grandma about my special surprise for mom. First, I had to answer all the usual 'grandma questions': Yes, I'd been a good boy; yes, I liked my new house; yes, I liked school; yes, I was making lots of new friends; and, yes, I missed her very much. Finally she asked the *one* question I could barely wait to answer! "So tell grandma, what are you giving mommy for Mother's Day?" Making extra sure mom was out of earshot so it wouldn't spoil the surprise, I whispered into the phone excitedly, "This morning before mom got up, I played with my erection set—daddy showed me how to make it even longer! After lunch I'm gonna take it out and let mommy play with it, too! Then we're gonna have sex together in the yard—just like the men across the street do!"

12

# THE BEE-WILDERED LITTLE PRINCESS
## Penny, 33

The only way I can admit to ever having been this incredibly naïve about sex is to relay this blooper in the same storybook way it unfolded in my young, innocent mind. Once upon a time there was a sweet, adorable princess (me—at five) who overheard her mother talking to her very beautiful eight-year-old big sister. The door to the sister's room was closed, which made the little princess even *more* curious about what was being discussed inside. So, she put her ear to the door and listened *very, very* carefully. Most of what she heard about birds and bees made no sense at all—especially since she couldn't see the pictures in the book her mother seemed to be reading from. Eventually, the little princess lost interest in what she couldn't understand and walked away.

A few weeks later, on a splendid summer afternoon, the princess's mother packed a delicious picnic lunch and took her two daughters for a lovely ride into the country. When they got to the family's favorite spot, she spread a beautiful yellow blanket under a glorious shade tree while the princess and her sister romped about picking berries and wildflowers. The sky was bluer than any the princess had ever seen . . . bluer than any color in her crayon box! Birds were chirping everywhere and the little princess was sure this was the happiest, most perfect day of her life. Little did she know how quickly things could get ugly! Out of the small bouquet of flowers she'd collected came an angry bumblebee. After buzzing around her head in dizzying circles, it landed on her bare midriff and stung the little princess on her rosy pink tummy before flying away. Alarmed, and in a good deal of pain, the startled princess dropped the flowers and began

13

*Alarmed and in a good deal of pain, the startled princess dropped the flowers and began to shriek at the top of her lungs!*

to shriek at the top of her lungs! Her mother and sister quickly rushed to her aid, both confused as to what was the matter.

"I don't want a baby! I don't want a baby!" wailed the little princess as her mother clutched her in her arms, confused as all hell over her shaken daughter's tearful despair. When the little girl looked down and saw her tummy begin to swell where she'd been stung, she became inconsolable, certain it meant the baby was already starting to grow inside her. Once again she began to shriek, "I don't want a baby. I'm too small for it to come out!" The little princess broke free of her mother's arms and ran for the car. Not until she was safely inside, with all the windows rolled up, did she begin to calm down. Her mother got in and sat beside her. Her voice was soft and reassuring, though, by now, she *too* was a total wreck! "Honey, can you tell me why on earth you think you're going to have a baby?" The poor, exhausted princess wiped her eyes and blew a big wad into the tissue her mother held under her runny nose. "Look," she said, and pointed to the small red lump just above her belly button. "I heard you saying things about the birds and bees. I listened through the door when you read the story to Betsy." The little princess continued to explain the facts as she naïvely interpreted them: If you heard birds chirping (which she had) and then a bee stings you (which it did), that meant you were going to grow a baby in your stomach. And, in *this* kingdom, this was *not* a good thing to have happen until there was a handsome prince and a big wedding *first!* Finally understanding, and truly relieved that her beautiful little child had not lost her mind, the wise mother thought for a moment and then smiled. "Oh, now I see," she said. "Then I guess you didn't hear the part about the ice cream." The pouting princess looked up into her mother's eyes and shook her head. "That's the best part," she continued.

15

"If a bee *does* sting you and you *don't* want to have a baby, all you have to do is buy your favorite flavor ice-cream cone and, before you take your first lick, rub the ice cream on the spot where you were stung. Then, you get to eat the rest of the cone." She leaned in close and whispered, "I hear it works even better with sprinkles!" On the way home they tried it and, lo and behold, it worked! From that day on, Dairy Queen (and her mother) held a very special place in the little princess's heart!

Many years later (after I'd met the man I would eventually marry), my mother asked me what form of birth control I was considering. I just looked at her and smiled. "I can't decide . . . vanilla or chocolate . . . but, either way, definitely with sprinkles!"

## THE STRUNG-OUT VIRGIN
### Kevin, 38

Whoever said, "a little bit of knowledge is a dangerous thing," must have been there the afternoon I *almost* lost my virginity.

My dad was a late-shift driver for a private ambulance company. Due to the often tragic and gory nature of many of the calls, my mom asked him not to discuss his job in front of us, fearing it would give us nightmares. Of course, what kid alive doesn't want to hear what he's not supposed to? So, one night, after my father came home, I sneaked out of bed and sat at the top of the stairs, listening to their conversation. Between fits of laughter, my dad described how they'd gotten an emergency call from a guy whose dick was stuck inside his girlfriend. The harder the guy tried to get it out, the worse things got. It seemed that she had her *period* (a word I'd never even heard, let alone understood) and was wearing a *tampon* (what the hell was *that?*), and the guy's penis got tangled up in her string. It somehow wrapped itself around and started cutting off circulation to his engorged organ. My dad and his partner wrapped the couple up in a sheet and took them to the hospital, still stuck together! There, the doctors cut him free. Of course, *I* assumed that meant they had to slice off the guy's dick! God, I thought, if this is what could happen when you have sex, I'm never, ever gonna have it! I never mentioned a word to my parents about overhearing the story, and kept all my convoluted impressions to myself.

Four years later, when I was 14, a few of my older buddies began to fool around with girls. One of them said he'd only have sex with a girl after he'd made sure there were no strings attached, saying, "Otherwise, they try and tie you

down and make you stay with them forever." I immediately flashed back to the story I'd heard my father tell years earlier, and once again I swore off ever having sex in my life! It just wasn't worth the risk!

Of course with my hormones raging, swearing off sex was an increasingly unrealistic expectation . . . especially when an older and experienced chick of 16 set her sights on me! One afternoon, while her parents were visiting relatives in the next town, she invited me over, supposedly to listen to music and stuff. It didn't take long before we were making out on her bed. I was already pretty worked up when she stopped and suggested we take all our clothes off. I'd never seen a girl completely naked, except in pictures, and the *real thing* had *my thing* standing straight out! She lay back on the bed, spread her legs, and pulled me down on top of her. "Oh, God" she said, "hurry up and put it in me!" As eager as I was to do just that, I was not prepared to risk life and limb!!! I was too smart to be tricked! Instead of following her orders, I slid down for my first up close and personal look between a girl's legs. Thinking back on that moment, she must have assumed I was preparing to go down on her, and she began squirming in anticipation, but my tongue never made contact. I just spread her lips as far as they'd go and peered as deep into her vagina as I could. Obviously tired of waiting and frustrated by my odd behavior, she pushed me away, sat up, and demanded to know what the fuck I thought I was doing. "Making sure there's no strings attached," I boasted proudly. "What the hell are you talking about?" she demanded. "How do I know that if we have sex I won't be trapped up there and tied to you forever?" By now she'd lost all patience with me. Totally disgusted, she practically threw me out of her house. "You're out of your fucking mind!" she said as she slammed the door in my face.

The next day in school she couldn't wait to tell *everyone* what a weird and strung-out virgin I was!

I guess my mother was right when she said my dad's stories might turn into nightmares. *This* one sure did!

# CHAPTER 2

# SEX AFTER SIXTY . . . 'ENSURED'

## GETTING IT ON OVER THE HILL

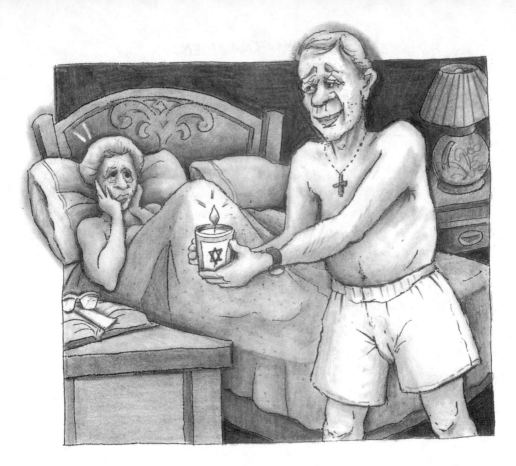

*In just a few minutes he returned to the bedroom—smiling so lovingly—with a glowing candle in his hand.*

# GRANNY AND HER 'GOY' FRIEND
## Thelma, 83

I heard about your book from my *meshuga* (crazy) granddaughter. So would you believe, something so private I never told a soul, now I'm telling you so that you can tell the world? I guess that makes *me* a *meshuggener* too! But, look, it's a crazy world we live in today and my granddaughter tells me I have to keep up. So, I'll tell you my story.

After going to sleep and waking up next to the same wonderful man for 57 years, who would think that just two years after I lost my beloved Sammy, that this Jewish grandma would find so much in common with another man? One from another faith, no less!

For months we kept company, going here and there. Frank was a widower and a perfect gentleman, not the way the young ones are today. He made me feel like a young girl again. So, I figured this way—*I* was 79 and *he* was 82—who knew how much more time *either* of us had? So, one night, I invited him to stay over. He was *so* pleased. I think he was afraid to ask me first.

Oy, we were both so nervous I was afraid one of us would surely have a heart attack right there! What should I do now? I was so *ferdrayt* (confused) I didn't know *what* to do next. Then I remembered a friend of mine, a widow herself for many years and a real maven in these things, saying she always used candles with a man because it made bodies our age easier on the eye. Since I live in Florida, where there are so many hurricanes, my daughter always makes sure I keep plenty of candles and matches under the sink in case of emergencies. I'm sure neither of us could have imagined *this* kind of emergency. When I suggested

23

lighting a candle to add a little romantic touch, Frank liked the idea and offered to get it. I gladly accepted, hoping it would give me a little time to quickly get undressed and slip under the covers before he got back. God forbid he should see me naked all at once! I told him just where they were, turned off the lights, and waited for him in the dark. I was so nervous . . . would you believe even *worse* than when I was a virgin! I'm sure *he* was plenty nervous too. He claimed he was faithful to his wife their whole marriage, so a playboy he wasn't!

In just a few minutes he returned to the bedroom—smiling so lovingly, with a glowing candle in his hand. It wasn't until he put it down on the nightstand next to the bed that I saw he had lit the *yahrzeit* candle I bought in remembrance of my late husband. Not being Jewish, what did *he* know from a *yahrzeit* candle? A candle is a candle! He had no idea this was *only* meant to be lit on the anniversary of a loved one's death. Can you imagine what was going through my head? It was killing me not to say something, but I convinced myself that this was God's way of keeping the memory of love itself alive. So, I decided to keep my mouth *shut* and my heart *open*. Now that's enough, don't ask me about the rest of the night. *That* much of a *meshuggener* I'm not!

# THE 'X' IN RX
### Tess, 74

You want to hear a little sexual blooper from someone over 60? Well, you've come to the right place! I'll let you in on a little secret: We lively ones call these our "assisted loving" years. I have to warn you—even with us sexier gals, it's not a pretty picture once these girdles come off! As the saying goes, "A little paint hides what the widow ain't"! I could tell you lots of funny stories. I'm proud to say my mind is one of the few things that still works on its own. I only wish the same was true of a certain part of my husband's body, if you know what I mean. Just when I'd given up hope and taken up needlepoint, a medical genius invents Viagra. I tell you, that was all you heard from people my age. Every other word was Viagra this, Viagra that. Everybody was running like crazy to their doctors for a prescription! To tell you the truth, the arts and crafts wasn't really doing much for me, so I convinced my husband that maybe we should see what all the fuss was about. Lately, I was up half the night anyway. You wouldn't hear me complain if he was *up,* too. I probably shouldn't talk like that, but how can I keep quiet now . . . I have to tell you the whole story.

All right, so *we* ran to the specialist too, like everybody else. He listened, looked at my husband's medical history, and gave him a big check up, including a prostate exam that my husband wasn't too crazy about. Men are such complainers! They should only have to see a gynecologist once a year. Anyway, the doctor said he would call in a prescription.

You can't imagine how embarrassed my husband was to pick it up. He waited for days! I told him he was crazy, and that no one cared what pills he took, but

25

that if it was so difficult I would go with him. Look, I figured *I* was gonna benefit from this too. What good would it do me if he never took them? So, just like the vows said, "for better or for worse," we walked up to the prescription counter together. The girl could hardly hear him because he whispered his name so low. He repeated it three times. Finally, I said it so she and the whole world could hear! While we waited for the druggist to fill the prescription, I figured I'd do a little looking around. At my age, you never leave a drugstore emptyhanded. Just as my husband was preparing to pay the cashier and quietly disappear, I raced up the aisle to the register. "Wait, wait" I hollered, and spilled a whole basket of laxatives and enemas onto the counter. "These are all on sale. Ring them up with his prescription." The cashier, a young girl of probably the same age as our granddaughter, began to giggle. I thought my husband would die! He looked like he wanted to kill me! Not one to mince words or become easily embarrassed, I put my cards—along with my money—on the table. "What can I tell you", I said, looking her straight in the eye, while my husband looked down at his feet. "*He* has trouble getting it up—*I* have trouble getting it *out!*

# THE AGING TOOTH FAIRY
## Arthur, 75

There comes a time in every gay man's life when he says "praise be" to a little lovin'—no matter how poor the timing! So, when my honey of 50 years (yes, 50) came prancing into the room where I was curled up with an unauthorized biography of the *faaabulous* Truman Capote in my lap and offered to give me a blow job—naturally, I put the damn book down!

Apparently, while I was in the throes of my good read, he'd been in his studio, reminiscing over a bunch of old photos taken of us during the summer we'd met on a beach in Mykonos. The two young men in the pictures were absolutely stunning specimens, certainly rivaling any model the Greeks had ever sculpted! "God", he swooned (in a tone I hadn't heard in more years that I care to admit). "You were *soooo* handsome . . . and *soooo* incredibly hung"! "I still am," I said teasingly, as I reached for his hand and placed it on my cock. I'm going to be entirely honest and admit we hadn't been terribly physical in years; so, when I did this, it was mostly just to be naughty. I suppose the images from those years stirred up the memory of all the hot sex we'd had, and put him back in the mood for love. Instead of playfully shoving me away (as I'd expected he would), he moved his hand up under my silk kimono and began masterfully massaging my still long—but mostly lost—friend!

I remember thinking to myself: Well now, *this* is certainly an unexpected surprise! Suddenly Truman Capote's life didn't seem all that fascinating. And, besides, I was sure *she* of all people would understand that a gentleman needs to strike while the iron—and his lover—is hot!

By now, dear Harold had managed to bring me to a glorious and full erection! I

frankly don't know who he was more proud of—himself or me! "Shall I finish you off in my mouth . . . for old times' sake?" he asked, with a spark of confidence I hadn't seen in years. "Obviously *I'm* up for it, if *you* are! Think you still got what it takes?" I teased. Ever thoughtful, I threw him a large pillow (listen honey, old knees are still old knees—no matter how inspired). With that, he knelt down and took me into his mouth. I was delirious with pleasure, when I began to sense that my little love slave was experiencing a bit of a problem—his feverish sucking was loosening his dentures! Too proud to stop, he gallantly continued until finally his uppers loosened *completely* and fell out of his mouth! The poor dear was mortified! To be perfectly honest, *I* was a bit shaken too. What had happened to those two mighty studs smiling back at us through time? Then, just when I thought his fragile ego was permanently crushed (along with my chances of cumming), Harold surprised me once again. Instead of feeling defeated, he reached into his mouth and *intentionally* removed his lower plate too, placing his full set of dentures right there on page 201 of Truman Capote's life! Without hesitating further, he took me back into his mouth and once again began sucking away.

Well honey, I have to tell you—this was a sensation no man should die without experiencing! For all the blow jobs I'd ever gotten in my illustrative youth, *nothing* had ever compared to *this!* Minus the choppers, Harold's mouth felt like a velvet-lined pump, creating the kind of suction you simply cannot get from someone with teeth. In just seconds, I came in his mouth. Now, with nothing about his performance to be ashamed of, Harold looked up at me with this toothless, shit-ass grin.

Who said you can't teach an old dog new tricks? You can keep all those gorgeous young hunks you see in the bars . . . just give me an old toothless fairy any day!

*Harold looked up at me with this toothless, shit-eating grin.*

# PAR FOR THE (INTER)COURSE
## Bill, 68

The first time I got my AARP membership card in the mail, I was convinced it was the beginning of the end. It was as if every part of my once vital body had been officially notified of my new, old status. My wife, who'd already come to terms with the lighter side of the inevitable, looked at retiring to Florida as a matter of course. To her way of thinking, every part of our bodies was already heading south, so we might as well pack up the rest of our things and go with them! The year I turned 65, we did. By the time we were issued our condo pool tags, I had become seriously depressed. That New Year's Eve, my wife told me I needed a major attitude adjustment and announced a joint resolution. She proclaimed that, beginning January 1, we were taking back our lives! Despite minor aches and pains, we would resume doing everything we *once* did—with regularity and enthusiasm—*including* having sex! Careful to count my blessings, I was grateful that that didn't call for a prescription of Viagra!

Like everything else that seems to take more planning and consideration in these less than spontaneous years, sex was no different. We couldn't do it in the morning because of her arthritis. We couldn't to it at night because that's when she liked to read in bed. We couldn't do it after her hairdresser's appointment because it would ruin her hair. We couldn't do it after a meal because the food would just "lay in her chest." The list of couldn'ts went on and on, and the window of opportunity became smaller and smaller. Finally, we negotiated some time after my morning golf game. I'd come home, shower, and, for as much as we cared to, we'd have a go at it. Afterwards, I'd take a nap and she'd hit the

malls before we'd meet up with the usual crowd in the usual places on the early-bird circuit.

Such was life in the old fart lane and, I suppose, compared to those who spent their time in doctor's offices and hospital rooms, I really couldn't complain. In the spirit of my newfound appreciation of the little things in life, one day I decided to take my camera to the golf course and shoot a bunch of pictures of me and my buddies playing a round. As I snapped away, I thought about which of us would be the first to drop dead, and I hoped it wouldn't be me!

A few days later, I took the film into a one-hour photo-processing center. I ran a few errands, then swung by to pick the pictures up. While the woman dug through the bin of envelopes to find my pack, we started up a friendly conversation. When I told her about the pictures I shot, she said *her* husband was a golf nut, and asked if I would mind if she had a look at my photos. Without going through them first, I gladly handed her the whole bunch. "So, how's your game?" she asked as she studied the photos, one by one. "Ah, what can I say—most of the time I'm usually too stiff." Suddenly her face changed as she stared at the snapshot in her hand. "Oh, my" she said, "it looks to me that, on *this* particular hole, *that* could be an advantage!" Puzzled by her remark, I leaned over for a look at what she meant. I turned beet red! Obviously I hadn't finished the roll on the golf course, and my wife, practical joker that she is, somehow managed to take a close-up photo of her own vagina with a small flag sticking up from between her lips. On it, she'd printed the words: BILL'S 19<sup>TH</sup> HOLE!

31

*His eyes flashed like he'd just discovered gold!*

## MR. FIX-IT
### Gloria, 66

God bless my husband. We've been married over 45 years and the man—a retired mechanic—can't stop fixing things! No matter what we're doing or where we are, if he sees something that's not working properly, it becomes his responsibility to try to fix it. It could be someone *else's* problem . . . it could be someone *else's* property . . . it doesn't matter. I'll admit, in the early years of our marriage, living with a man like that was a dream come true. I was the envy of all my girlfriends. When something would need repair in their households, all the husbands would ignore their complaints. *Mine* couldn't wait to have a look. Even after a long day at work, nothing made him happier than to come home and putter in his workshop.

Sadly, the one thing my husband *couldn't* fix was our sex life! I was becoming less and less interested and, not surprisingly, so was he. It wasn't that I didn't want to anymore—in fact, I actually missed it—it was just that after menopause, my vagina was much drier, even when I was aroused. That made intercourse uncomfortable and, at times, even painful. When I told my gynecologist about the problem, she said it was fairly common among older women. She recommended I purchase a tube of K-Y jelly, a lubricant that seemed to work wonders for everyone who tried it. At first, I felt a bit inadequate about needing such a product, especially remembering back to the days when my husband would practically drown in my juices! But, I figured, what the hell! Eager for results (and a much-needed orgasm), I bought a tube immediately. That night, I put on his favorite perfume, my sexiest nightgown, and dimmed the bedroom light.

33

When my husband finally came upstairs, I was ready for him. "Come here, you," I said in my sexiest voice. "Something under this gown needs fixing and I understand you're the man with just the right tool." At first, he seemed a bit reluctant, not wanting to repeat our earlier disasters. I assured him that this time would feel as good as it used to, and he quickly undressed and got into bed. Hoping to work it into our foreplay, I produced the tube and explained its use. He got excited all right, but *not* in the way I expected or hoped, and certainly *not* in a way that did *me* any good!

"Wow," he said as he read the label, "I wonder how many *other* uses this thing has that nobody's ever thought of?" With that, he jumped out of bed, squeezed some out and ran it along the metal track of a sticky dresser drawer. When it slid smoothly, his eyes flashed like he'd just discovered gold! He squeezed out another wad and pushed it into the old hinges of our squeaking closet door. When that worked too, he pulled the ladder over to the bedroom ceiling fan and squeezed some of the lubricant directly up into the mechanism between the blades. Then, he turned on the fan and, much to his delight, no more clicking sound! By now he was completely turned on . . . by the K-Y jelly—not by *me!* "This stuff's great," he raved, "they should sell it in the hardware store next to the WD-40!"

There I was, feeling totally neglected while my husband ran all over the house with the tube, applying the jelly to everything he could think of. By the time he remembered *me,* and returned to the bedroom, there was barely a drop left. Everything in the house was lubricated and humming, *except for me!* I was the *only* thing still bone dry and, needless to say, my mood was way beyond repair!

34

# CHAPTER 3

# PAGES FROM THE FAMILY ALBUM

*THOSE MEMORABLE MOMENTS YOU'D RATHER FORGET*

## *MOMMA'S BOY*
### Tammy, 34

When I hit my thirtieth birthday a few years back, I started dating with a new attitude. Hoping to settle down (preferably sooner than later), I made up my mind not to go out more than once or twice with anyone I didn't think had potential. Since most of the guys I'd been dating were great in bed but otherwise complete jerks, that automatically ruled out pretty much everyone, leaving me with more time on my hands than I ever wanted, or needed.

After a very long dry spell, I finally met a fairly normal guy, through a fixup of all things, which only goes to show you how desperate I'd become! Now, I wouldn't exactly call him Mr. Right; he was more like Mr. Possible and, with the right kind of training, maybe even husband material. Unfortunately for me, the thing he needed the *most* training in was sex! While he certainly wasn't lacking in the meat department (thank God for small—and large—things), he was a total amateur when it came to oral sex. This was particularly troublesome, since that just happened to be the thing I enjoyed the most!

I tried to be patient and mature about the whole thing. If he was willing to put aside his male ego and learn a thing of two, how could I not be willing to teach? After literally months of licking and tonguing lessons, I came to the sorry conclusion that he was hopeless! By then, I'd grown to really like the guy, especially since he was so sincere about trying to please me. Most of the time I just faked it, so we could finish without hurting his feelings. I knew I couldn't keep up the charade much longer, but I didn't quite know how to break things off so close to his fortieth birthday. I was only praying he wouldn't use the occasion to

propose, and guilt me into marrying him. Grateful that he didn't ask during dinner, I was more than happy to accommodate his amorous overtures, especially since I knew in my heart it would be the *last* sex we'd have.

So, there he was—frantically (and still uselessly) trying to apply every technique he had failed to master—when, suddenly, the phone next to his bed rang. Truly believing he had me on the verge of cumming this time, he was too determined and too well mannered to consider interrupting my pleasure. On the third ring, the answering machine picked up. The call was from his mother. While *he* remained entirely focused on pleasuring me, *I* was paying more attention to her message. She said she was calling to wish him a happy birthday . . . and say that she missed him so much, she made her husband pull out all the old home movies of him growing up. Obviously, there were quite a few scenes of him as a baby, fussing in his high chair as she tried unsuccessfully to feed him. "Oh, honey," she cooed into the telephone, "you were the cutest, most adorable little thing . . . but, God help me, you were *such* a poor eater!" I swear I don't know what came over me, but when I heard her say that, I reached over and picked up his phone, interrupting her message. "Hi," I said in this really nonchalant tone, with her precious little boy still between my legs. "I'm Tammy, your son's soon to be ex-girlfriend, and I just thought you should know that he's *still* a poor eater!"

# CAT'S GOT YER TONGUE
## Ted, 49

It's never easy meeting your girlfriend's family for the first time and, even though she warned me how odd many of them were, *nothing* could have prepared me for it!

Abby and I, both in our thirties, had been dating exclusively for months. Shortly after I officially moved in with her, she found out she needed a partial hysterectomy. It wasn't the *best* news in the world, but it certainly wasn't the *worst*, at least, not for us. Her mother, on the other hand, could not be dissuaded from racing up from Florida to be with her child. Being of a different faith, I soon learned that that's just what a Jewish mother does! Anyway, the compromise was that she'd come up *after* the surgery and spend a few weeks in the apartment caring for (and annoying the hell out of) her convalescing daughter.

The surgery went well and, before long, my future mother-in-law descended upon us with more luggage than anyone going on a three-week cruise would need! Packed in a well-padded suitcase all its own, sat a bizarre, three-foot ceramic cat that she'd proudly glazed all by herself in an arts-and-crafts class. She was convinced it was *just* the decorative touch her daughter's living room needed, so she schlepped it all the way up to New York and positioned the tacky monstrosity in the corner beside the recliner. She also decided that what Abby needed was some company, so she called every relative still living in the tristate area and invited them over for a Sunday brunch. Abby told me it was a waste of energy to fight her mother on this, and that I should go pick up some deli while she donned a new bathrobe and combed her hair to receive her guests.

39

By late afternoon, the apartment was packed with relatives. Each and every time someone else arrived, Abby's mother would repeat the details of Abby's condition. In between all the talk about her reproductive organs and private parts, *I* was introduced as "the boyfriend."

As the conversation (and noshing) wound down, I found myself sitting beside Abby, being stared at by a roomful of strangers. For an uncomfortably long time, no one knew quite what to do or say. Just when I was certain the tension couldn't get any thicker, Abby's matronly grandmother (who up 'til then had been quiet) looked up from her lap and stared directly at me. "So, Ted," she piped up from across the otherwise silent room, "what do you think of Abby's new pussy?"

It felt like I was literally suspended in this desperate state of disbelief, when suddenly, in a moment of recognition, Abby burst out laughing. She patted me on the arm reassuringly and pointed to the corner of the room. "It's okay sweetie. Grandma is referring to the beautiful ceramic cat that my mother made for me!" Completely unaware of how her question sounded, it was *grandma's* turn to be flustered and confused. She leaned over to her niece and asked innocently, "What did he *think* I meant"? With that, everyone under sixty-five in the room keeled over in a fit of uncontrollable laughter!!!

# THE OFF-COLOR COLORING BOOK
*Coleen, 48*

Coming of age in the sixties, I could have been the poster child for the entire hippie generation. From psychedelic drugs to promiscuous sex, I did just about everything that, today, as a mother, I'd cringe to think of my own daughter trying! And yet, as radical as I was (and, in many ways, still am) it didn't prevent me from falling madly in love with a young corporate executive and settling into the comfortable bourgeois life I'd spent so much of my youth rebelling against. It was no secret that my strong liberal and feminist views, along with some bisexual experiences, made me *less* than his extremely conservative and, as far as I was concerned, repressed parents' favorite pick for a daughter-in-law!

I became obsessed with gaining their approval, and turned my first child into a proving ground! I was determined to get my in-laws to admit that, despite my fringe values, in all the important areas of parenting, my sense of discretion and sound judgment was above reproach! My daughter must have sensed how much I had riding on her because, by the age of five, she'd managed to completely charm the pants off everyone—including her impossible grandparents—and finally earned me the long-awaited credit I felt I deserved. Unfortunately, due to one innocent little *faux pas*, all my credibility turned to shit!

It was an otherwise uneventful Sunday afternoon, and my in-laws had dropped by for an informal barbecue. While my husband and his father fired up the grill, my mother-in-law and I worked side-by-side in the kitchen, shucking ears of corn and preparing a salad. Quickly bored with helping us, my daughter complained that she wanted to do something that was more fun. I came up with

41

*My daughter's face beamed with pride while my mother-in-law's expression turned to horror!*

several possible activities, but they only drew pouted lips. Close to being at a loss, I reminded her of her crayons and coloring books and suggested how nice it would be if she colored some special pictures just for grandma. *That* idea thrilled her and she skipped off to her room to do just that. She was gone quite a while when my mother-in-law and I decided to look in on her progress. With proud smiles, we delighted in watching her from the doorway of her room as she feverishly scribbled away, turned to a new page, and began all over again. Eager to offer her praise, my mother-in-law walked over to her little table for a closer look. I saw my *daughter's* face beam with pride while my *mother-in-law's* expression turn to horror! I couldn't imagine what was wrong, until I took a closer look for myself!

With all the dozens of fairy tale and Disney-themed coloring books at her disposal, it seemed my precocious little girl had somehow found my copy of *The Joy of Sex,* a big, soft-covered book complete with page after page of large black-and-white illustrations depicting nude couples engaged in every possible sexual act in every possible position imaginable (many of which I was quite sure my mother-in-law had *never* seen before, let alone *tried!*). Oblivious to the subject matter, my daughter mistook its format for just another coloring book with lots of pretty pictures of nice men and women playing together.

Well, color *me* crimson red, and my *mother-in-law* a sickly green! As embarrassing as it was, I suppose it could have been even worse—my daughter *could* have pulled out the companion book, *The Joy of Lesbian Sex,* and colored in *that one* instead!!! No crayon in the *world* could have captured my mother-in-law's color *then!*

# THANKSGIVING LEFTOVERS
### Teri, 37

After saving for ten years, my lover Denise and I finally bought a house and moved out of our tiny one-bedroom in the city. I don't know who was happier to have a real backyard—us or Josephine, our feisty little schnauzer. Everything reeked of *Ozzie and Harriet*, especially our white picket fence.

Since this was going to be our first Thanksgiving in our new home, we thought it would be nice to invite our families for the holiday, something we never had the space (or the guts) to do before now. Since this was going to be a big first for us in our relationship, and we were hoping it would further validate the normalcy of our life, we went to great lengths to make it unforgettable. We sent out special invitations, planned a traditional menu with lots of combined family favorites, and raced to get the house in shape for its first official showing. Having just moved in six weeks earlier, there was *much* too much to do and *much* too little time to do it, so we decided to focus *only* on what would show. We shoved lots of miscellaneous unpacked boxes anywhere we could find space.

Finally, Thanksgiving arrived! Everything looked perfect . . . unless you opened one of the closets or peeked under our bed. Our relatives started arriving by the carload; parents, grandparents, aunts, uncles, cousins, our siblings and their kids. In many cases, they would be meeting each other for the very first time. Denise and I were both nervous. Naturally, things were a bit awkward and tense at first, but after a few drinks and tours of the house, everyone from eight years old to eighty seemed to have found a reasonably comfortable place for themselves in our living room. At that point, I thought it was safe to excuse myself and help Denise in the kitchen. With

44

the sound of conversation flowing from the room, we took a moment to share a victory hug and a huge sigh of relief. Everything was going even better than we had expected.

All of a sudden, a deathlike hush fell over our entire home. Except for Josephine's playful barking, you could hear a pin drop. Denise and I rushed into the living room to see what was happening. Her grandmother had both hands over her mouth as if to suppress a gasp, our sisters used every hand available to cover their children's eyes, and everyone else just gaped in utter shock. There, in the center of the room, surrounded by 26 of our closest relatives, was our dog waving a 12-inch double-headed rubber dildo in her mouth! Obviously, she'd found our sex toys in the shoe-box we temporarily shoved under our bed. By the shape and feel of it, she must have figured it was a new chew toy that she'd never seen before. Hoping to get someone to join her in a playful tug-of-war, she pranced around the room, dropping it at various people's feet, growling and pouncing on it with both paws. Horrified, Denise screamed out her name in the most blood-curdling voice I'd ever heard her use. The dog, scared for her life, dropped the dildo and ran . . . leaving the lifeless thing just lying there on the floor. No one moved a single muscle as I walked over to it, smiled meekly, and picked it up.

Truthfully, I don't know how *any* of us got through dinner after that. Suffice it to say we certainly had a lot of leftovers, but *nobody* asked for a doggie bag! It took Denise and me weeks to get over the whole ordeal, and I had to convince her not to put the dog to sleep. It certainly wasn't the quaint little Hallmark celebration we were going for, but somehow we all managed to survive . . . all of us, that is, except for poor grandma. We told ourselves it was just a horrible coincidence that she had a massive heart attack and died, one week later. I swear, on our double-headed dildo, that's the truth!

45

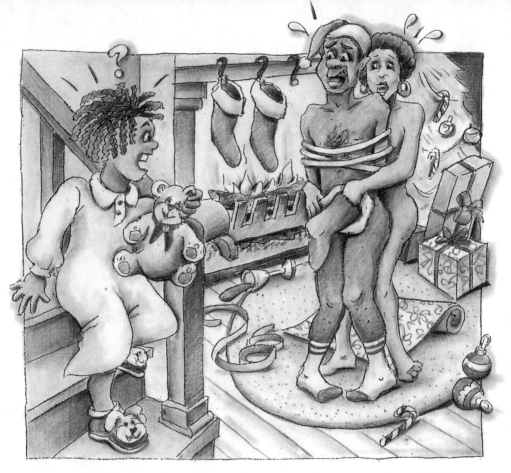

*My quick-thinking wife—still reeling from the moment—reached up and yanked Allison's stocking from the mantle.*

# JINGLE BALLS
## Anthony, 36

It was the night before Christmas. Only after she'd hung her stocking, drawn a picture for Santa, and put out some cookies, would my five-year-old daughter, Allison, consider being tucked into bed. Once that mission was accomplished, my wife and I waited a while to be sure she'd actually fallen asleep before we began gathering up all her presents we'd hidden around the house. While my wife got into the holiday wrapping, I put on her favorite Johnny Mathis Christmas CD, and poured us the first of many glasses of eggnog. We wrapped and sang and drank for hours and, by the time all the presents were stacked around the tree, we were both more than a few sheets (of wrapping paper) to the wind!

Feeling a bit horny, I searched through the box of holiday decorations until I found the mistletoe. Then, I chased her around the room, held the mistletoe over her head, and kissed her passionately. No doubt turned on by the effects of all the eggnog as well as my tongue, she took some rolls of unused ribbon and playfully tied my hands behind my back. I could already feel *my* 'chestnuts' begin to roast while she made me watch her suck the stripes off a candy cane! Then she pushed me up against the wall next to the mantle, unzipped my fly, lowered my pants and dropped to her knees in front of me. I was just on the verge of cumming, when I looked up and saw my daughter standing at the bottom of the steps, watching us curiously. Obviously, she'd heard noises coming from the living room and, naturally, thought it was Santa. Instead of catching *him* giving out presents, she caught *her mother* giving me head! What could I do? My hands were tied—in every sense of the word!

47

"Where's Santa?" my daughter demanded. Horrified to hear Allison's voice, my wife scrambled to her feet, leaving my fully erect cock totally exposed! Obviously more *annoyed* with us than *upset* by what she saw, Allison reprimanded us both: "You *have* to come to bed *right now*—Santa won't leave me my presents until everybody's sleeping"! Then she put her hands on her hips and stared disapprovingly at my penis. "Daddy, why do you *always* have to wear that thing?" Having seen me naked on a few different occasions, and having compared *my* body to that of her own and her mother's, she must have assumed my penis was some sort of accessory that I could either put on or take off at will. Already annoyed with me for interfering with Santa's visit, she was *really* upset at seeing it *this* time. My quick-thinking wife—still reeling from the moment—reached up, yanked Allison's stocking from the mantle and pulled it up over my cock, trying simply to remove it from our daughter's sight. What seemed like a resourceful move instantly made matters worse! "No, Mommy!" my daughter shrieked. "Get it out! Get it out! I don't want Daddy's thing in there! There won't be any room for Santa to put my candy!"

As if that wasn't traumatic enough, let's just say Rudolph's nose paled by comparison to the color my wife and I turned when we overheard Allison describing her ordeal to a roomful of shocked relatives gathered for Christmas dinner the next day. Judging from everyone's faces, X-mas had suddenly taken on a whole new meaning!

# CHAPTER 4

# PETS WILL BE PETS

## THE UNTAMED SIDE OF ANIMAL BEHAVIOR

# MY UNFORGETTABLE CAT-ASTROPHE
### Jill, 38

Unlike just about every other lesbian in the world, I absolutely *hate* cats! That being said, I was not terribly thrilled to learn that this woman I had the hots for had not one, not two, but *three* of her own! Since all I could think about was getting closer to *her* pussy, I had no choice but to put up with the *others*, especially since she had her own place and I still lived at home.

After just making out on our first few dates, she finally invited me to spend the night. As excited as I was, from the moment I set foot in her bedroom I knew I was in big trouble. As we started to undress, I became short of breath. Not realizing I was having an allergic reaction to all the hair balls and dander, I thought I'd suddenly developed some sort of performance anxiety, and was having my first panic attack! Totally embarrassed, I managed to convince her (and myself) that my noticeably heavy breathing was because of how turned on I was by her naked body and the idea of making love to her. Believe me, if *that* hadn't been true too, I'd have been dressed and out of there in a flash! Instead, I crawled into her bed and focused on the one pussy I was there for, trying my best to ignore the other three.

In a vain attempt to get one of the cats to stop licking my toes while I was doing some serious licking of my own, I jerked my foot, hoping to knock the damn thing off the bed. Instead, he retaliated by clawing half my leg! Seeing how annoyed I was, my girlfriend managed to round up two of the three and lock them out of the room. She convinced me to let the third cat stay hidden under the bed, assuring me that he'd remain there and not get in our way. Still inter-

ested in pleasing this woman any way I could, I foolishly agreed, and resumed my position between her thighs. I will admit that watching *her* mounting pleasure made it easier to ignore *my own* mounting pain from the welts forming on the back of my leg. Suddenly, I felt the cat jump up onto the bed. (So much for her assurances!) I tried to get him *down* while still trying to get her *off*, but there was no way I could take care of two pussies at once! Sensing my distraction, my girlfriend begged me to just ignore the cat. With the goddamn animal now sitting on my back, that was a lot easier said than done! Just as I had her moaning and groaning, the damn cat began gagging and heaving! The very same moment my girlfriend exploded and creamed into my mouth, the cat exploded and vomited into the crack of my ass!!!

All I could think about was getting revenge, and believe me when I say that in the 'cat fight' that followed, I made sure he used up *all nine* of his lives! Satisfied at having gotten my licks in (all around), I was definitely outta there— *fur* good!

# A LITTLE BIRDIE TOLD THEM
## Gwen, 42

I don't know where the fixation came from but, ever since I can remember, I've had a thing for parrots. Even though I'd begged my parents for one the way most kids beg for a puppy, the closest I'd gotten to anything with wings was a parakeet from the local pet shop that wound up croaking in just five weeks. Then came a replacement canary, which lasted even less time than that! I finally told my folks to just forget the whole thing, and promised myself that as soon as I grew up and had a place of my own I would get the parrot I'd always wanted.

Somehow, the years flew by and, after I graduated from my small hometown college, I announced my decision to move to New York City. Needless to say, my overly protective parents weren't thrilled, especially since I was an only child. They were certain that my strict moral upbringing would be shot to hell living in a city of so much sin! I'd never dared admit that, for *me,* that was a big part of the draw! Instead, I went out of my way to assure them that my morality (and hymen) would remain intact! Wanting to be supportive and trusting in spite of their grave misgivings, once I'd found a job and an apartment, they bought me a handsome, yellow-headed parrot as a housewarming gift.

Seymour was the sweetest thing! We bonded immediately and became the best of friends. Despite the fact that I'd taught him to welcome me home with "hello, gorgeous," his affectionate little love pecks were no substitute for the real thing. Since having left the nest, I was more than ready to spread my wings, *and thighs!* After becoming a regular on the singles' scene, I met a really great

guy, Brian, and finally started having some really great sex. In hindsight, I guess Seymour *saw more* than perhaps he should have.

Anyway, it was long after I'd lost my virginity that I found the nerve to tell my folks I was actually *dating* a guy. Hoping to avoid their disapproving lecture, I lied and told them we'd met in the culinary section of a bookstore (when, in fact, it was really at a pool table in a local bar). Foolishly, I went on to brag about what a great guy he was and somehow got roped into inviting them down for a taste of my new boyfriend and my new life. As unprepared as he was for meeting the folks, Brian was willing to play along when I asked him to act like a ridiculous prudish kind of guy who would never *dream* of deflowering me . . . their innocent little virgin . . . before marriage!

So, there we all were, sitting around in my living room sharing our views about the moral decline of society, when Brian (obviously caught up in our little charade) decided to lean over and plant a virtuous little kiss on my cheek. Mistaking *that* as the start of our usual foreplay, Seymour squawked as clear as a bell, "Oh yeah, fuck me good!" Before I could leap to my feet and do damage control, he launched into a barrage of x-rated phrases I had absolutely *no* idea he'd learned: from "suck my cock" to "fuck me harder baby"! Seeing the look on my *parents'* faces when he screeched, "Oh God, I'm cumming!" all *I* could think was, "Oh God, I'm dead!"

54

*I guess Seymour saw more than perhaps he should have!*

# MUTT-TERNAL INSTINCTS
## Craig, 34

I was dating a woman who thought of her dachshund more like her *child* than her *pet*. Not only did she feed it from a baby bottle and bathe it in an infant's tub, she actually dressed it in yellow boots and a slicker when it rained. It even had its own baby blanket and photo album! Now ordinarily all this crap would have totally turned me off, except that everything *else* about her turned me on! Figuring the way to her heart—and bed—was through her dog, I went out of my way to pretend that *I* found the scrawny thing as adorable as *she* did. Eventually, all the squeezie toys and rawhide I bought paid off, and I was finally going to get *my* bone sucked! While she changed in the bathroom, I made spitefully sure that every stitch of clothes I tossed off wound up on top of the dog. By the time he managed to crawl out from beneath my Jockeys, I was in bed—ready and waiting to fuck his mistress. Since he was too pathetically short to jump up on the bed and get in my way, I figured I'd let him hang around and enjoy the show!

Because this was our first time and I wanted to come off as a sensitive lover, I decided to put *her* needs before *mine*. What she wanted most was for me to go down on her, which I was more than happy to do, figuring she'd have to return the favor. Now, I don't like to brag, but if there's one thing I know for sure, it's that I'm great at chick licks! Usually, I can get a girl off in less than three minutes, often timing myself in my head to see if I can break my own record! For some reason, she was taking forever and I was beginning to wonder if I'd ever get *my* turn! Eventually, she came, but then she said she had to pee and freshen up. After that, she just wanted to cuddle and talk. While I tried to be obliging,

56

*conversation* was not exactly the oral gratification I was looking for! Finally, she sensed that she wasn't playing fair. My ball(s) were in her court, and it was time for her to return the serve . . . and the service! As it turned out, she was every bit the player that I was and knew how to beat me at my own game. Several times she sucked my cock to the point of cumming, but then deliberately slowed down to hold me back. My balls were aching and this time I needed her to go all the way. Once again she worked me to the edge, but just as I was about to shoot my load, the dog suddenly keeled over and went into some kind of epileptic fit, making really gross sounds and foaming all over my clothes! Totally panicked, my girlfriend jumped off *my* twitching thing and began stroking the one lying on the *floor!*

We spent the rest of the night in the emergency room of an animal hospital. It was obvious that by the time the *crisis* was over, so were my *chances* for having a few good spasms of my own!

57

*In a cruel twist of fate, my best laid plans—and best loved pooch—both went up in smoke.*

# A SHOCKING TAIL
## Ling, 54

Years back, when I lived alone, I thought it would be fun to own a dog—you know, for the companionship and all. After looking around, I got hooked on a wire-haired fox terrier, a breed often described as "a small dog with a big attitude." As soon as I spotted him among the others in the litter, it was love at first sight. Built somewhat on the slight side, but considerably feisty myself, I instantly identified and bonded with the most adorable little eight-week-old pup. Despite our many clashes of will, not to mention his often cantankerous behavior, he became the absolute love of my life! As independent as we both were by nature, we were virtually inseparable. No matter what I did, he was there, which ultimately turned out to be *not* such a good idea!

I had my precious for three wonderful years when I went out and got myself something *else* I soon became instantly attached to—my first vibrator! This was quite a few years ago, back when there were a lot fewer cordless models to choose from. And, it came with more attachments than you could shake a stick—or dick—at, but since the latter wasn't always accessible on a regular basis, the purchase seemed a really practical alternative.

While I couldn't have been *more* satisfied with my new little pleasure machine, it was quite obvious from the start that Toby the terrier did *not* share my enthusiasm! Much to the contrary, the buzzing annoyed the hell out of him, especially when I'd alternate the settings between high and low to maximize the effect, but there was no way in hell I was going to let a dog come between me and some of the best orgasms of my life! I tried locking him out of the bedroom

when I used it, but hearing the noise through the door only incited him more and he would bark like a mad dog the whole time. At least when I let him stay in the room with me he kept his agitation down to a low growl. At the time, it seemed like the lesser (and quieter) of two evils and more than a reasonable compromise. He would lie there and growl from the floor alongside the bed, while I lay there and moaned from on top of it!

This one afternoon, with our understanding in place, I got out the vibrator and we took our respective positions. As usual, I plugged in, turned on, and expected to get off. Only *this* time, in a cruel twist of fate, my best laid plans— and best loved pooch—both went up in smoke. It seemed that while *I* was on my back, groaning away, *he* was busy gnawing away on the electrical cord. Eventually he chewed his way down to the live wire, and when his wet mouth made contact with the current running through it, he not only short-circuited my orgasm, but also shocked himself in the process! Imagine *my* shock! While *that* wasn't exactly the climax I was hoping for, fortunately the shock didn't actually kill him and the only replacement I had to buy was a new *vibrator*—not a new *dog*!

# HOT DOG!
## Mark, 42

When I met Sandy, it was love at first sight—and lust at first sound! What I mean is, the woman of my dreams turned out to be 'a screamer' . . . the type that's very loud during sex. When she cums, the whole building relaxes with a cigarette afterwards! While I admit this was a bit embarrassing at first, it proved great for my male ego—leaving no doubt in *my* mind (or the *neighbors'*) that I must be one helluva lover! The one problem was that my screamer owned a yapping Pomeranian—and a jealous one at that! When it came to my girlfriend's affection, he and I were definitely rivals. If *I* put my arm around her, *he* offered his paw. If *I* kissed her on the cheek, *he'd* lick her on the other. On more than one occasion, immediately after she and I had our usual screaming sex, the dog tried to attack me. One time, he actually broke my skin with his teeth! To add insult to injury, she scolded *me* for smacking her precious pooch, even though it was in self-defense! This had become a real bone of contention between us and I was only slightly comforted in knowing that, although the dog was the *other* love of her life, at least *I* was the one fucking her!

We'd been dating for about three months and, hoping to make our first Christmas together really romantic, I rented a cozy cabin for us in a ski resort. Unfortunately, 'just the *two* of us' became the *three* of us when she informed me that she couldn't bear the idea of boarding the dog. The place was great! Just as the owner assured me, it had the three things I was looking for: proximity to the slopes, a balcony with a view, and a huge stone fireplace. The bearskin rug was an unexpected treat and we couldn't wait to make love on it!

61

While she changed into a really sexy little number, I popped open the champagne and got a roaring fire going. Just as I dreaded, the minute we got down on the floor the dog became a royal pain in the ass! Totally pissed off, I insisted she lock him in the bedroom for the rest of the night. The next few hours, he yapped his goddamned head off and scratched at the base of the door while she and I polished off the champagne and caviar and did 'the wild thing.'

After a while, she had to pee. When she got up to use the bathroom (which was inside the bedroom), I figured I'd rebuild the fire, which by now had died down to just a few, smoldering embers. I removed the screen and was bent over (butt naked) stoking what little remained of the log, when suddenly I sensed the dog charging at me! From the corner of my eye, I saw him take a flying leap at my jewels. All I could think of, when I saw those exposed fangs, was to get out of his way and protect my balls! With precision timing, I jumped off to the side and, a split second later, the dog landed right in the fireplace. Hearing its cries, my girlfriend ran into the room just in time to see her weenie roasting! *This* time, her screams sounded *very* different from those before!

In response to her shrieks, I reached into the fireplace, pulled him out, and rolled him in a blanket to smother his burning fur. After making numerous phone calls, and driving God knows where for God knows how long, we finally got seen by a vet. Though the pads of his paws were a little raw and patches of his fur were singed, the doctor assured my girlfriend that, with a little TLC, the dog would be just fine.

Nevertheless, that was the end of *our* romantic weekend! *She* spent the rest of the time with the mutt in her arms while *I* ended up getting screwed—doggie style!

# CHAPTER 5

# PARTY OF ONE

## WHEN MASTURBATION INVITES DISASTER

*Every morning after breakfast, I'd stand quietly by while she wrapped this wide black band around her arm.*

## LAST WILL AND TESTICLE
### Herman, 36

I was a typical 13-year-old, freckle-faced kid the summer I went to visit with my grandparents. They lived in a really huge house not far from a lake, and it didn't hurt at all that the most beautiful girl in the world lived just down the block! All of 18 herself, she seemed really developed and, from the moment I laid eyes on her, she instantly became the center of my fantasy life. Since I'd just started masturbating a few months before, I now had a real live girl to picture naked whenever I jerked off. Between fishing trips with my granddad and matinees with my grandmother, *that* was something I did *a lot* that summer!

Something *else* that captured my boyhood imagination was a strange contraption my grandmother used to take her own blood pressure each day. Every morning, after breakfast, I'd stand quietly by while she wrapped a wide black band around her arm. Then, she'd squeeze a rubber ball at the end of a hose, until the band gripped her arm tighter and tighter. Eventually, she'd release it and the band would gradually relax. The whole thing kind of spooked me, but I was really curious to know what it felt like. So, one day, while my grandmother was asleep on the couch and my grandfather was at the store, I sneaked into their bedroom, went into her closet, and took out the mysterious machine. Having memorized the steps I'd seen, I wrapped the band around my scrawny forearm, then pumped and released over and over.

After repeating this cycle several times, I began to wonder if I hadn't just discovered another way to masturbate! Eager to try out my new invention, I dropped my shorts and wrapped the band around my penis—then, pumped and

released, pumped and released, as fast as my little fingers could squeeze! I couldn't believe how good it felt to have something *other* than my own hand wrapped snuggly around my throbbing little cock. Certain that I would soon ejaculate, I grabbed a wad of tissues so I wouldn't shoot all over grandma's favorite hooked rug. Unfortunately, I never got that far because, much to our mutual horror, she walked in on me! I can only imagine what her blood pressure would have been had she taken it just then! Just when I thought she was going to have a stroke, my grandfather returned. Quickly assessing the matter at hand, he sternly escorted me out, and told me to wait in my room while he tried to calm my grandmother down. I can't imagine what they said to each other, but neither ever said another word about it to *me.* Thank God I only had another few days left to my visit, and I was more than grateful that, for the rest of their lives, it was *never* mentioned again.

After a long illness, my grandmother died when I was 21. My grandfather passed away much more suddenly, nine years later. Since his estate was sizeable, the whole family was called together for the formal reading of his will. After reading through page after page of legal mumbo jumbo, the lawyers solemnly pronounced my grandfather's special requests. Among a short list of possessions, he bequeathed the following items: his wedding band went to my *older* brother, his gold watch went to my *younger* brother, and my grandmother's blood pressure kit went to *me!* Never one to forget a thing, my grandfather's obvious intention was to leave *each* of his grandsons something of sentimental value to wear!

# A LONG TIME CUMMING
## Yolanda, 35

I know there are lots of women who think of masturbation as a means to an end—that end being an orgasm, of course. They treat it like an unromantic quickie. Personally, I have always preferred to wine, dine, and otherwise pamper myself before going all the way. I remember this one time my own hand was *so* good to me I actually went out the next day and bought it a ring!!! But, like all love affairs, even the ones you have with yourself, sometimes it's not always wine and roses!

One afternoon I found myself very much in the mood for love and, as usual, went to great lengths to indulge myself. I luxuriated in my Jacuzzi, prepared a candlelit dinner for one, and popped open an expensive bottle of wine. Afterward, I stepped in front of a full-length mirror, slipped out of my long silk robe, and began seductively applying deliciously scented lotion all over my naked body. It had now been several hours since I began my dance of self-love, and I was eager to finally surrender to my mounting desire! With my favorite romantic ballads playing softly in the background, I lowered myself onto the satin sheets and slowly began making love to myself. I closed my eyes and indulged my fantasy, imagining that I was being forced by my captors to make myself cum. Between all the wine and my stroking, I was rather *high*—and rather *hot!* I moaned (in character, of course), begging them to let me go, while naturally I ignored my own pleas and continued to bring myself closer to the humiliation of cumming while they watched.

67

Just as I was about to have the most delirious orgasm, I inhaled some of my own saliva and seriously began to choke! *Unwilling* to stop rubbing and *unable* to stop coughing, I now had a life-and-death decision to make! Hopelessly gagging, I had no choice but to stop. Frustrated beyond words, I sat up and caught my breath but, after so much coughing (and so much wine), I had a raging migraine! Still too stubborn to accept the fact that all my preparations had gone to waste, I tried once again to get myself off, but the more I rubbed, the more excited I became, and the more excited I became the harder my head pounded until I was sure *it* would explode before *I* did!

Annoyed as hell with myself I finally gave up, slapped my own hand, rolled over onto my side and mumbled at it threateningly, "Not tonight dear . . . I have a headache!"

# MOM'S X-RATED ZZZs
*Janis, 31*

As a divorced, working mother with a big house and two boys (two and five years old) to take care of, it's an understatement that I don't get too many chances to tend to my own personal needs without a million interruptions. So, when my neighbors offered to take my older son to the amusement park I was forever grateful, and all but shoved him into their overcrowded van. With my little one finally down for his afternoon nap and a few precious hours all to myself, I frankly didn't know what to do first! I quickly dismissed the dishes in the sink, the laundry in the bin, and the pile of paperwork on my desk and opted for a luxurious bubble bath instead. Submerged in the silky bath oil and surrounded by lovely scented candles, I actually began to fantasize. It wasn't long before I was pretty aroused and was ready for something else—namely, my pathetically *underused* vibrator!

I peeked into the nursery and, with my son still soundly asleep in *his* bed, I hurried off to *mine*—spread out a towel, then my legs! As I reached into the back of my drawer for my vibrator, I nervously checked the clock. It was heaven knowing it would be hours before my son would be home! Since I hadn't had sex for an embarrassingly long time, my body craved the stimulation and I made myself cum at least a half-dozen times. Now totally relaxed from my multiple orgasms, I was suddenly overcome with fatigue. I guess I must have unintentionally drifted off into an uncommonly deep sleep.

I was still sleeping soundly when my son arrived home (sooner than expected, because one of the kids had gotten sick). Since I was often busy and

69

couldn't easily get to the door, I'd recently taught him *not* to ring the bell but to use his big-boy key and just let himself in. With all the things I've had to nag him about, that's the *one* damn thing he listened to! My neighbors watched to make sure he'd gotten in safely before they pulled into their own driveway just down the block. Once inside, my son must have looked for me in all the usual places and, when I was nowhere to be found, marched upstairs. When to his surprise (and my regret) his innocent little eyes found me totally naked and sprawled out on my back with the small, silver vibrator still in my hand, he came to his own horribly mistaken conclusion! The poor kid was too panicked to even scream (which obviously would have awakened me then and saved me from humiliation)! Instead, he ran straight out of the house and down the block to my neighbors. When they came to the door, he was crying uncontrollably and saying things like, "Mommy's in her bed! She's dead! The gun killed her!" While my girlfriend kept him safe and called 911, her husband grabbed a baseball bat and raced over to my house. He sneaked up the stairs quietly, just in case an intruder was still there. Of course, the only thing he found was an obviously safe (and satisfied) woman napping!

I don't know who was more rattled when I suddenly opened my eyes and gasped at seeing him standing there gaping at me. *He* was quick to explain what he was doing there, as *I* nervously threw on my robe. Staring at the 'weapon' lying on the floor, he smiled and said, "I guess you're not dead!" Totally humiliated, I scooped the thing up and shoved it into my pocket just as the squad car arrived. "No, I'm not dead," I thought to myself, "but right now you can't imagine how *badly* I wish I were!"

70

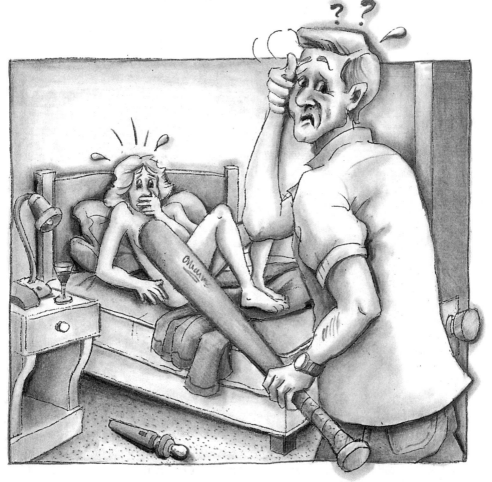

*I don't know who was more rattled when I suddenly opened my eyes!*

## COMING CLEAN
### *Rochelle, 42*

It started out like any other bath for a kid my age—strictly a parentally enforced ritual. In my 12-year-old mind I figured, the faster *in* the faster *out,* so I could get on with the more fun stuff in life! So, there I was, halfheartedly cleaning myself down there when, quite by accident, I began to experience the most pleasurable tingling sensation. The faster I rubbed, the wetter I got and the better it felt! My breathing quickened, my pulse raced, and, all of a sudden, my flushed young body exploded in the most incredible wave of pleasure I'd ever known. *Wow!* I never knew *anything* like that *existed,* let alone that it had a name. What a fantastic discovery! I wondered if anyone *else* knew about this wonderful thing. For a moment, I just lay there in the empty tub. I was exhausted but thrilled to have stumbled upon such a fantastic secret! My exuberance soon turned to panic when I realized that I didn't know what the hell *it* was or how the hell I got *it* to happen! Sensing that this was not something I should ask my mother about, I desperately feared never being able to duplicate my special feeling again!

I tried not to appear overly anxious to take my next bath. (It never even occurred to me that I could have that feeling somewhere else . . . in my innocent mind, I actually thought the bathtub itself had something to do with it!) Once behind the closed bathroom door, I struggled to collect my thoughts, desperate to re-create my unnamed state of bliss. When I concentrated, the thing I seemed to recall most vividly was how mysteriously slippery the inside of my vagina had gotten, and how good that made it feel as I rubbed. That's when it hit me—*soap*

72

always makes things slippery! All I had to do was use the soap to get that feeling back! Thrilled with my problem-solving skills, I wet the soap, resumed my spread-eagle position in the tub, and began rubbing the slippery bar as hard and as fast as I could over a part of my anatomy I later learned was called a *clit*. At first, everything was going great! All those incredible sensations were coming back and I was definitely headed in the right direction. All of a sudden something went *very* wrong—terribly, painfully wrong! Instead of recapturing that wonderful tingling, the little mound of flesh where I was concentrating all my efforts began to burn like hell! My clit had become so engorged and raw it was like rubbing soap on an open wound! Confused and utterly defeated, I finished my bath the old way and got out of there as quickly as I could. I spent the next several hours trying to conceal my pain and downright despair. I was absolutely miserable and totally convinced that my botched attempt meant I would *never, ever* get to experience that sweetest of sensations again.

Resigned to my terrible fate, I was prepared to live out my long, pleasureless life without so much as another try . . . that is, until one afternoon when my mother tended to my badly scraped knee with a fingerful of Vaseline. A little light bulb suddenly lit up in my head, and from that day (and jar) on, I lit up regularly between my legs!

*While the whole congregation looked on, I spent the most miserable morning of my life.*

# THE 11TH COMMANDMENT: THOU SHALT NOT SQUISH
### *Jules, 27*

Having convinced my parents to let me attend a regular public school when both my older brothers were enrolled in private yeshivas, there was *no way* I could get out of at least being bar mitzvahed! So, the minute I turned eleven, I was sent to Hebrew school in preparation for my official coming out . . . as a Jewish man! The truth was, by the second week of classes I was more convinced than *ever* that the only two things worth praying for were that the Tom Cruise rumors were true and that I'd never get caught masturbating—especially since I'd begun to jerk off pretty religiously! Sometimes, I'd do it alone in the bathroom, and sometimes with a friend in the woods. Sometimes, my erections weren't even intentional, but those were just as hard to ignore! Considering all the pressure I was under with my regular schoolwork, my Hebrew lessons, and my secret obsession, I thought I was handling myself pretty well! After a couple of intense years of Hebrew (and homo) lessons, my big day (or should I say my *parents'* big day) arrived! On the morning of my bar mitzvah, I was in my bedroom studying my naked body in front of the mirror when, in an obvious act of God, my cock sprang to life! In what could either be interpreted as a supreme act of stupidity or a mighty leap of faith, I convinced myself that I could jerk off and *still* be ready to leave for temple on time. So, there I sat, legs apart, staring at a poster of a barechested Tom Cruise as I pumped my dick. The very moment I started to cum my mother suddenly knocked on my door! Naturally, I panicked! Not knowing what to do, I reached down, grabbed one of the shoes, shoved myself into it

and finished ejaculating into the front of my brand new wingtips! Nervous as all hell, I told her to wait a minute while I quickly cleaned myself off and threw on my freshly pressed pants. With my knees still shaking and my heart still pounding, I opened my door. My mother, all dressed for temple, beamed with pride! Surprised to see that *I* was nowhere near ready, she held out the jacket to my new dark suit and hurried me along. Now fully dressed except for my shoes, I stood in my stocking feet while my mother straightened my tie. She reminded me how proud she was and how I'd soon be taking the most important step of my life (yeah, especially with my *right* foot, I thought)! "Okay, honey", she ordered, "now put on your shoes and let's go." Leaving nothing between my poor toes and a pool of sticky semen but the hope of some divine intervention, I took a deep breath, clenched my teeth, and slipped my feet into my shoes. By the time I finished tying my laces, the front of my right sock was soaked with the stuff of my manhood!

While the whole congregation looked on, I spent the most *miserable* morning of my life reading aloud from the Torah (while cringing inside). When the service was *finally* over, the rabbi congratulated me but, by *then*, it was really hard to give a shit. Maybe in the eyes of *God* I'd become a man . . . but, in the tip of my *shoe*, I'd become a gooey mess!

# CHAPTER 6

# SCREWED, BUT GOOD

## THE BIG 'WHOOPS' IN A LITTLE WHOOPEE

# A MAN-'MAID' DISASTER
## Rina, 37

For the last 12 years, I've been married to a man who's extremely detail oriented about everything, including our sex life! When it came to his sexual fantasies, he would go to all kinds of extremes to create realistic scenarios. It wasn't enough to just *act* them out—we'd have to be in *full* costume, using *real* props. On this one particular occasion, he even insisted we go on location!

The fantasy I'm talking about went like this: He's a wealthy business tycoon who, while staying at a very posh hotel, gets serviced by the beautiful chambermaid sent to make up his room. To act it out (for the sake of authenticity), my crazy husband actually booked a suite in one of the city's most expensive hotels and got me a sexy little French maid's uniform (complete with duster) from a place that rents theatrical costumes. The plan was that, on the morning after we checked in, I was to pretty myself up, squeeze into my skimpy costume, and leave the room while my husband showered. About 15 minutes later, I was to return and let myself in with our room key. Once inside, I would be surprised to find him just getting out of the shower and offer to come back at a more convenient time, but he would insist I stay and just go about my duties. After watching me bend over to make up his bed, he would become aroused and surprise me from behind with a full erection. Pushing me down on the still unmade bed, he would pull down my panties and mount me doggie style. After he came, he'd offer me a large tip to let him taste me and cum in his mouth. Then, grateful for the best oral sex I'd ever had, I would use my feather duster to tickle him back into another full erection and then suck him dry in my mouth!

Well, that's what was *supposed* to happen! Instead, while I was waiting outside the hotel door, the real maid was pushing her cart down the other end of the corridor. She obviously thought that I was using a disguise to gain entrance to the man's room for the purpose of robbing him, because she immediately notified hotel security. They arrived at our door and started knocking, just moments after my husband had penetrated me from behind. Since they didn't announce themselves, we assumed it was just the real maid and, because we had the DO NOT DISTURB sign on the door we simply ignored it. Now, even *more* aroused by the close call, my husband urged me to keep my moaning down as he continued to thrust faster and faster. Just as he was about to cum, the lock suddenly clicked and our unchained door swung open. In burst two security agents along with the maid who pointed at me and said, "That's her!" Mortified, I ran for the bathroom and locked myself in while my husband took the agents aside and explained what was *really* going on.

Overhearing the conversation and all their laughter, I quickly gathered that the agents were fully expecting to catch me in the act of burglarizing my husband's room. Unfortunately, the only act going on was me being mounted from behind. As soon as the men were gone, you can be *sure* that I treated my husband to the unfeathered end of his fantasy . . . and my duster!

# CABIN FEVER
## Damian, 28

As a hot, up-and-cumming young porn star whose credentials more than stood out in a crowd, I soon realized I was wasting my time cruising the local bars when I could be discovered cruising around the Mediterranean in high style with a much older (and richer) jet-setting producer I'd recently met at a party. While I preferred to think of myself as his personal cabin boy, I knew that, for those next three weeks, I would be just another working stiff, and that all hands on deck would really mean all hands on *dick—his!*

Now, it didn't take too many stolen glances to realize that hot young gay men staffed half the cruise ship! So, every night, after I *fucked* and *tucked* my producer in, I'd go hang out with the guys down below. Since he had no real interest in me personally, this didn't seem to bother him at all, as long as he got his blow-by-blow description of my nightly escapades. Sometimes he wanted to be sucked off before breakfast, which was okay by me. Sex always made me hungry and his two little poached eggs and sausage were just starters for me!

About a week into the cruise, my producer cast me in a leading role. He told me to borrow a uniform from one of the boys and, when he ordered room service later that night, *I* was to bring the tray to his cabin. Once inside, I would get propositioned into staying and having sex with him for a considerably generous tip! He thought the whole thing would be more exciting for him if he spent the earlier part of the evening alone so, right after dinner, we went our separate ways. I was to be ready—in uniform—to take the tray from the kitchen to his cabin when he called in his order, precisely at midnight. With my costume

81

secured and several hours left 'til show time, I sat in the lounge and let the handsome hunk of a bartender pour me *way* too many drinks! Luckily, I'd told him about my midnight performance so, at 11:55, he pointed me in the direction of the kitchen and told me to break a leg. As drunk as I was, it was amazing I didn't do *just that* as I raced downstairs to change into my uniform. A friend in the kitchen who was in on the plan quickly filled the order and handed me the tray. I honestly don't know how I made it up in the service elevator without dropping the whole thing! As I stood in front of the cabin door, with no one else in sight, my instincts as an actor told me to improvise. So, just before knocking, I put the tray down, pulled out my cock and worked myself into a starring nine-inch erection. Then, I picked up the tray, knocked on the door, and announced myself. When no one answered, I knocked again, and eventually a really old guy in pajamas and slippers opened the door. That's when I realized I had the *right* cabin—but the *wrong* deck! (Even when I was stone cold sober, all those goddamned floors and corridors looked exactly alike!)

The old guy took one look at the tray and called out to his wife, "Rhoda, did you order room service?" "Are you crazy, Murray?" the old woman called back from their bed. "What would I be eating *this* hour of the night?" With that, he glanced down at my impressive erection and just shrugged. "Sorry, young fella, but you heard my wife." Then he lowered his voice and whispered, "If my memory serves me, you're about 30 years too late!"

*I knocked again and eventually this really old guy in pajamas and slippers opened the door.*

# DADDY'S (NOT SO INNOCENT) LITTLE GIRL
## Michael, 33

I recently married a wonderful girl who, despite her very strict and sexually repressed Irish-Catholic upbringing, turned out to be a real tiger in bed! Although she wanted to stay a virgin until we were married, after the wedding, she was determined to make up for lost time!

The whole time we were dating, her parents (especially her father) kept a close eye on me—making absolutely sure I wasn't messing around with their little girl. Since my new father-in-law was a retired cop who made no bones about still having his revolver, I didn't dare try anything with his daughter that would cause him to use it! Kathleen's mom was just as much a fanatic when it came to her daughter's reputation. My wife and I joke about how pathetic her parents' sex lives must have been. We could never imagine them doing it in anything other than the same, boring missionary position. With five other siblings, Kathleen was sure that her mother had had more *kids* than *orgasms!*

Luckily, my little bride was going to see to it that *her* sex life would be anything *but* average, and our honeymoon would be her sizzling introduction to it all! She made me promise that we'd try everything there was to try and that we'd capture it all on video so she could go back and watch herself getting fucked over and over again. I loved the idea (and the irony) since it was her parents who bought us the camcorder so we could capture the wonderful memories of our honeymoon in Hawaii . . . which, by the way, they *also* paid for!

Kathleen made me take the camera *everywhere* we went and shoot hours and hours of god-awful tourist attractions. On a whole separate tape, we also shot hours and hours of our more private honeymoon memories, and we shot some pretty wild stuff! After viewing the tapes, even *I* was impressed with our performance!

Unfortunately, our honeymoon flew by and, as soon as we got back, my wife became overwhelmed with the stress of her new job and our new home. Wanting to give her one less thing to think about, I offered to dupe the sightseeing tape and mail it off to her parents even before they started nagging her for it. Trying to be a thoughtful new son-in-law, I enclosed a personal note along with the cassette labeled OUR UNFORGETTABLE HONEYMOON. On the inside of one of our engraved thank-you cards I wrote, "Dear Mom and Dad—Hope you enjoy *watching* this as much as your little girl and I enjoyed *making* it!"

The rest is *sin*-ematic history! It wasn't until a couple of days later, when my sweet little pineapple and I sat down to some hot Hawaiian porn and piña coladas, that I suddenly realized I'd made a terrible (and unrewindable) mistake! Somehow, I mailed off the wrong tape!!! Once I admitted what I had done, my wife couldn't decide whether to divorce me or simply kill herself! When I foolishly pointed out that the church condemned *both* those acts, she was quick to remind me that *that* didn't seem to deter us from all the *sins* we committed on the tape! Since we hadn't yet heard from her parents, she thought there *still* might be time for a miracle—so she went to church to pray.

Now, I'm not easily impressed but, two days later, the package was returned to us—unopened—for insufficient postage!!! When I asked her what she had promised God in return, she looked at me with this ball-busting expression and said, "I promised never to have any *other* kind of sex but intercourse . . . and *only* in the missionary position!"

85

When the phone finally rang I was pumping away and real close to cumming.

## CONVERSATION INTERRUPTUS
### Neil, 41

After going out with my now ex-wife for over a year, we decided to live together. The good news was that the sex was intense! The bad news was that the sex was intense! How's that possible? I'll tell you. My ex's job required her to travel a lot, which meant that while she was home we pretty much fucked every night but, when she was out of town, our bodies felt like they'd gone cold turkey! To ease some of the pain, her nightly check-in calls from wherever she was would quickly turn into really wild phone-sex sessions. We'd lay naked on our separate beds and take turns masturbating while we described everything we'd do to each other the next time we were in the same room together. While some of those calls got pretty damn hot, one left me in an ice-cold sweat!

Sheila had already been gone for three full days when she called from her hotel room on the East Coast. In a very sexy voice, she told me she'd had a little more than usual to drink over dinner with some business associates and that all she could think about was getting back to her room so I could do her over the phone! Not that I didn't appreciate the chance but, as it happened, I was expecting a call from a buddy of mine who was supposed to be getting back to me about unbelievable courtside tickets to a Lakers home game! Let's face it—a guy can cum just about anytime, but a chance for courtside seats only comes along once in a lifetime—if he's lucky! So, even if she *did* have all three fingers shoved deep inside her, and even if my cock *was* as hard as a rock, when I heard that call-waiting signal there was no way in hell I was going to let it go! Instead, I made up some bullshit about expecting an important business call from a really big

87

client, and asked her to hang on while I confirmed our meeting. Pumped with excitement (about the game), I pressed the flash button to switch over to the incoming call, only to hear my ex-mother-in-law's voice! That's when I was *convinced* that God had to be a woman and that every chance she got, she fucked with a guy's head (and, I don't mean the one on the end of his prick)! Hoping to end the conversation quickly, I made the mistake of telling her I was on the phone—long distance—with her daughter. Instead of letting me go, she asked a million damn questions about how she was, and gave me a whole song and dance about how much she hated the idea of her daughter bouncing around the country so much. The only way I could get rid of her was to promise I'd have her daughter call her back right after we got off!

I don't know what happened but, when I clicked back to my ex I realized we'd been disconnected. While I waited for her to call back, I put the time (and my hand) to good use. When the phone finally rang I was pumping away and real close to cumming. With my free hand, I lifted the receiver and started describing how hard I already was and how badly I wanted to cum in her mouth! As my voice faded into the moans of a desperate man undoubtedly jerking himself off, I'm sure I heard my ex-mother-in-law gasp and hang up!!!

I couldn't believe it! The whole time I'd been describing how I wanted to cum in my ex's *mouth,* and instead, I wound up cumming in her mother's *ear!*

## OOPS AND THE UPS MAN
### Pamela, 36

I'm one of those women who always finds a guy in uniform a real turn-on. Maybe that's why I fell madly in love with and married the UPS guy whose route included the accounting firm where I worked as a receptionist. For me, it was love at first signature! During our brief courtship and early years of marriage, our sex life was all flares and rockets. But, as time went on, he seemed more interested in football than foreplay and, before long, his indifference spread to me. That's when I knew we were in big trouble! He was reluctant, but I finally got him to sit down and talk about our issues. As much as I usually resented his immediate tendency to problem solve his way through everything in life, I must admit that, in *this* particular case, I rather liked his approach. Since his uniform had been such a turn-on for both of us in the beginning, he came up with the brilliant idea of pretending to be a UPS guy who I'd get to fuck me while my husband was away at work! The plan was that he'd leave the house early and, then, sometime later that morning he'd return, in uniform, and call from the intercom in the lobby to announce a delivery. I would buzz him into the building and wait for him to ring our apartment door. That's when I would get to play out one of my all-time favorite fantasies—that of a sex-starved housewife, forced by her frustration to seduce the deliveryman.

My husband's next day off was a Wednesday. I could hardly wait! According to plan, he left the house while I was still asleep. When I woke up, I found a note on the kitchen counter saying that he'd be working late that night, as usual. In anticipation of my unexpected delivery, I took an extra long time in the shower.

89

By then I was already so turned on just by thinking about it, I had to fight my urge to masturbate. Instead, I convinced myself that remaining frustrated would only make my fantasy seem more real. I forced myself to just go about my normal routine but, this time, in only a bathrobe and a touch of perfume. Finally, the lobby buzzer rang (after I'd checked the clock every 10 minutes for nearly two hours). I hurried over to the intercom box in our front hall and asked who it was. "United Parcel," a man's voice crackled back through the tiny speaker of the box. "Okay," I said, and buzzed him in. Fortunately we lived on a very high floor, which gave me a little time to change and get into character. In my fantasy, I always came to the door in a small, loosely wrapped towel that just happened to come undone and fall to the floor while I signed for the package. Naturally, at the sight of my luscious body (which I *do* have) his massive cock would go rigid inside his pants. Embarrassed by his obvious erection, *he* would awkwardly try to hide it behind his clipboard while *I* would make no attempt to cover up! Instead, I'd announce that my indifferent husband wouldn't be home for hours and invite him in to fuck me any way he'd like!

I was already soaked with excitement by the time the elevator reached our floor. Then came the actual knock on the door. "Who's there?" I inquired, just to be sure. "UPS," a manly voice rumbled back. With my heart—and cunt—pounding beneath my skimpy towel, I unchained the lock and opened the door. Standing there in full uniform, with a package and his electronic clipboard in hand was *not* my husband, but an incredible hunk with a *real* delivery . . . and a *real* interest in his eyes!!!

Before I got a glimpse of where *else* his interest showed, I quickly slammed the door in his face! "Please, just leave the package and go," I pleaded in an obviously shaken voice. "No problem," he said as he put down the box. I swear, I could hear the amusement in his voice as he added, "Don't worry, I know about the fantasy all you women have. Unfortunately for *me*, you're not the first who wouldn't let me deliver!"

# CHAPTER 7

# ONCE UPON A TRYST

## WHEN THE STORY ENDS UNHAPPILY EVER AFTER

# THE BUZZ AT GARDEN GABLES INN
### Bernice, 51

My husband and I, though both confirmed East Coast city slickers, have always loved being in the great outdoors, especially during autumn. Every year, to celebrate our October wedding anniversary, we set some time aside to spend a long romantic weekend in upstate New York, surrounded by the breathtaking splendor of the colorful foliage. We always stay at a different bed and breakfast each year, usually one recommended by friendly locals. Though the old wooden floors tended to squeak and the plumbing was often antiquated, we much preferred the ambiance and charm of those magnificent Victorian houses to the sterile blandness of those awful roadside motels.

As much as we enjoyed mingling with the other guests around the delicious home-cooked breakfasts each morning, we savored our anniversary weekend nights alone, when we'd retreat to our cozy bedroom and make wild, passionate love with all the enthusiasm of the newlyweds we once were. I should mention that, at the beginning of *every* September since we were married, my usually clean-shaven husband would grow a beard. It was his rustic mountain man statement. Invariably, by December, he'd be sick of it and, on January first, he'd shave it off. As crazy as it sounds, I've always found this temporary change of his to be sexually arousing, because it felt like I was suddenly in bed with an entirely different man. I've found myself more sexually adventurous during those months, and, recently, I even suggested we introduce some sex toys into our lovemaking. So, on our first night of our weekend, when my husband surprised me with a beautifully wrapped gift and a lovely anniversary card, I was thrilled to open it and find he'd gotten me a sleek,

state-of-the-art vibrator! I was so excited I could hardly wait to try it out and, when I did, the sensations were beyond *anything* my poor deprived clitoris had ever known! I made him use it on me so many times I was afraid we'd wear out the batteries on the first night! Of *all* the presents he'd ever given me, *this* little thing was definitely the best! Needless to say, the next morning over breakfast I was in a glorious mood, but I sensed that the elderly woman who owned the place was studying my husband rather suspiciously. When he said he hadn't noticed, I shrugged it off and didn't give it another thought. We spent *another* wonderful day antiquing along scenic back roads, enjoyed a romantic dinner in a cozy corner booth, and, upon my plea, skipped dessert so we could hurry back to our room and my wonderful new toy! This time, I convinced my husband to let me try it on him as well and, between all the combinations and attachments, we had a "buzz on" through most of the night!

The next morning, we once again joined the other guests at the table for breakfast, and, once again, I noticed the owner staring curiously at my husband. This time her scrutiny was so thinly veiled that even he was aware of her preoccupation. I was determined to find out what was going on. After breakfast, I took her aside and, in the privacy of a small room off the main hall, I questioned her about it. "I was just wondering," I said in a discreet whisper, "is there something in *particular* about my husband that concerns you?" Her eyes filled with a peculiar mix of reservation, and relief at having been asked to explain. "I just can't understand it" she said, obviously very confused, "He *still* has a beard!" Now *I* was the one totally confused. "Why wouldn't he?" I asked. "Don't you hear him? For the past two nights he's been up all hours shaving with his electric razor and, *still*, every morning, he has the *exact* same beard!"

96

# MY (NOT SO) SECRET CROSS-CUNTRY AFFAIR
## Eleanor, 47

As an executive sales rep for a software company I'm required to attend national trade shows. As much as I've never mastered the art of smiling at thousands of buyers for the sake of potential business, there was one time a few years back when my smile came quite easily! It was nearing the end of the second of a three-day New York City show and, after standing around for hours in my sensible pumps and black Donna Karan suit, all I could think about was getting back to my hotel, changing into a comfortable pair of jeans, and heading down to the West Village to my favorite girl bar. Since I was (more or less) happily married to a really nice guy for the last fifteen years, and hadn't been with a woman since my college roommate, hanging out with lesbians in a gay bar thousands of miles from home seemed the safest way to reconnect with my alternative side.

Just as I was preparing to leave the convention center, the most exquisite woman I'd ever seen approached the booth and smiled directly at me. This time, my face lit up naturally. I almost knocked over the other sales rep in order to answer any questions this woman had about our product line. My only regret was that we weren't selling dildos and vibrators because I *sure* would have liked to help her with *those!* Instead, I remained professional and focused, which wasn't easy because she was uncharacteristically charming and effervescent for a buyer, and it soon became obvious that *she* was flirting with me!

We both took more than casual notice of one another's wedding bands, but didn't let that dissuade us from continuing our conversation over dinner. As we shared our pasts, she confessed that she'd never actually been with a woman but

97

*That's when we heard the unexpected sounds of people clapping and cheering.*

had been curious for years. When she spotted *me,* she said, she could no longer resist the temptation. Sensing my interest as well, she decided to throw caution to the wind. Amazingly, we discovered we were both staying at the same rather small hotel uptown. However, so too were many others in town for the same show, who like us, preferred the intimacy of a less glitzy place. After several drinks and slow dances at a smoky lesbian bar, we shared the most tantalizing tongue kiss, and she told me she couldn't wait for us to be alone in my room! We thought it safer to take two separate cabs back to the hotel and walk through the small lobby separately. I'd been a repeat guest for several years and was known by pretty much everyone on the staff. Neither of us had ever done *anything* like this in our marriages before this night, and we were extremely fearful about being seen together.

Once back at the hotel, I waited anxiously for my beautiful buyer to come to my room. I was beginning to think she'd had a change of heart when there was a knock at the door. I opened it up, looked both ways down the center hall and then pulled her inside. Our first few searching kisses evoked more desire than either of us had *ever* known. We could barely come apart long enough to undress and fall onto the bed. Drunk with the thrill of being in each other's arms, we rolled around in an intoxicating mix of playfulness and passion. As we continued to explore the secrets of each other's bodies, our girlish giggles soon gave way to womanly moans. After thrashing around in a frenzy of positions, we wound up locked in a heavenly 69 and soon cried out within seconds of each other!

That's when we heard the unexpected sounds of people clapping and cheering coming from the telephone receiver on the night table. We must have acci-

dentally knocked it off the hook! Much to my horror, I remembered that in *this* hotel, all you had to do to get connected to the front desk was just lift the phone. As I slammed the receiver back down on its cradle, I couldn't be sure whether their phone system indicated *which* room the sounds were coming from!

Checkout the next morning was possibly the *worst* ordeal of my life! As I stood nervously at the front desk and paid my bill, I *couldn't* (and *wouldn't*) meet anyone's eyes. *Did* everyone know . . . or *didn't* they? Just when I'd convinced myself that I was being unnecessarily paranoid, the assistant manager accepted my room key, looked up, and smiled from ear to ear. "It's always nice to see you," he said, "do come again!"

# FROM HERE TO EMERGENCY
## Mel, 75

My wife and I met right before I was drafted into the army during WWII. I saw a lot of action overseas (some of it pretty bad) and, a lot of times, the only thing that kept me going as bombs flew over our trenches was thinking about the girl I left behind—and the action I'd see if I made it home to my honey. Her letters were a godsend, and I was a soldier in love! I even proposed marriage in a poem I'd composed in my foxhole. She's kept it for 50 years, God bless her.

I was one of the lucky ones and, not long after D day, I got shipped back to the states—all in one piece. Times were hard and jobs were scarce, but we were in love and wanted to be together. So, against our parents' wishes, we ran off and eloped. Back then, most nice girls wouldn't have sex unless they were married and, after coming through the war, there was only so much hardship a fella could endure! So, *she* got the ring around her finger and *I* got her lips around my you-know-what! Once we'd made it official, it seemed we went from little more than necking to doing *everything else* overnight. Not that I'm complaining—those were my glory days and I could stand at attention for hours! The more she wanted, the more she got. I'll tell you, that first year of our marriage was one of the *best* of my life. Hard times never felt so good!

In those days, going to the movies was a big pastime. Musicals and love stories were the most popular, and my wife dragged me to see every last one! Without a doubt, the one that made the biggest impression on her was *From Here to Eternity* with Burt Lancaster and Deborah Kerr. After seeing that famous

101

love scene, where they're lying together on the beach under the moonlight, that's all she wanted *us* to do!

Key West was not exactly a Hawaiian paradise, but it was as close to a tropical setting as we were gonna get on a tank of gas and very little cash. We parked as close to a deserted stretch of beach as we could and had to climb down a fairly rocky area to get to the sand. We'd packed some sandwiches and even splurged on a bottle of wine that we polished off as we watched the sunset. As night fell, I collected some driftwood and built a small fire. Huddled together, we couldn't wait for the stars to come *out* and our bathing suits to come *off!* Now, back then, they never showed you the movie stars naked, but you always got the idea. I soon found out there were plenty of *other* things they didn't show you in the movies either—and I'm not even talking about the fishy smell on the beach at night! For instance, they didn't tell you how terrible it feels when you get sand in the crack of your behind, or even worse, up her privates when you're trying to get yourself inside. It's awful for both of you, just plain awful! They also didn't show you the seaweed that comes in with the tide and how it could get tangled up in a woman's hair, or the crabs that crawl all around your naked body. But, worst of all, they didn't show you those poisonous Portuguese man-o-war jellyfish that get washed ashore by the waves. No, they sure as hell didn't show you *that!* So, there I was trying my best to give the missus the love scene she wanted, when one of those jellyfish washed up between my legs and stung me on the inside of my thigh. I never felt burning like that in my life! When I realized it'd come within inches of my balls, I knew I'd had enough! I didn't come through the invasion of Normandy to have it end *here,* on the shores of my own country! I grabbed my trunks and told my wife that *she* could stay and wait for Burt

Lancaster 'til the sun came up, but *I* was getting the hell off that beach!

With all my discomfort I still considered *myself* the lucky one because, when we climbed back up over the rocks in the darkness, my *wife* stepped barefooted right into a pile of dog crap! As for *our* big Hollywood love scene, like they say in the movies, "The End!"

103

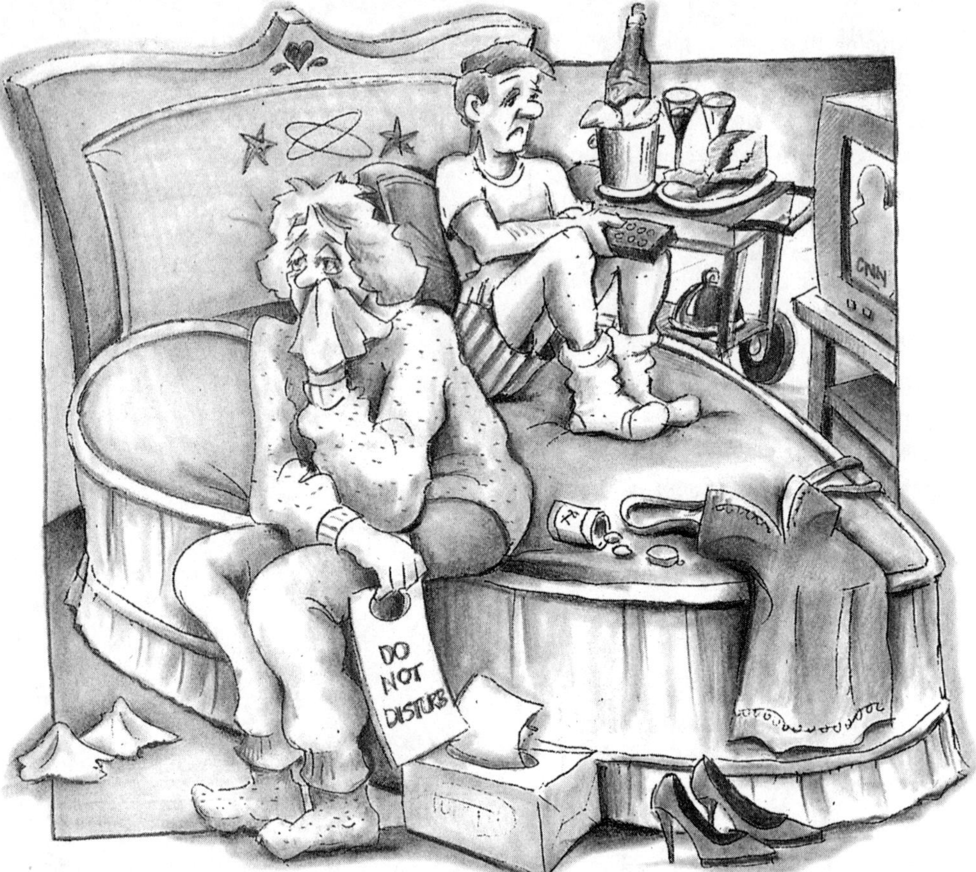
DO NOT DISTURB
CNN

*My wife was so drowsy from all the medication, she collapsed onto the heart-shaped bed.*

# BEST (UN)LAID PLANS
## Scott, 42

It's amazing how many things can go wrong when you try to make things right. That's just what happened when I surprised my wife on our tenth anniversary with second honeymoon plans. She'd been complaining for a while that the spark had gone out of our marriage and that, most of the time, she felt like I took her for granted. Since that really wasn't the case, I wanted to show her what a romantic fool I could *still* be and how much I really *did* love her. To prove it, I got my sister to watch our two kids for our anniversary weekend and booked us into the grand honeymoon suite at a resort that catered to couples—you know, the ones that advertise the tacky heart-shaped beds and private Jacuzzis right in the room. I even ordered her favorite flowers and a bottle of chilled champagne for our arrival.

I should have known the plans were doomed from the start when my wife came down with a touch of the flu the day before we were set to leave. She pumped herself full of antihistamines and insisted I take her anyway. Now *you* try to have a romantic weekend with someone who's warned you in advance that there'd be no mouth-to-mouth contact for fear of spreading germs! Since she still had *another* set of lips to work with, I foolishly believed *all* was not lost. Denial had always served me well!

By the time we arrived, my wife was so drowsy from all the medication that she barely noticed all the special touches before collapsing onto the heart-shaped bed and dropping off into a dead sleep as I lay there beside her—resigned to watching CNN. She awoke several hours (and many news updates) later, feeling somewhat better. She suggested we order room service and, after

105

she changed her mind at least a dozen times, we finally ordered two lavish lobster dinners. Of course, as soon as the serving cart was wheeled into our room, all the food smells immediately made her queasy. So, she called back for some crackers and plain broth that she slurped from *one* side of the room, while I devoured both lobsters from way over on the *other!* Between her coughs and sniffles, we sipped champagne and toasted our love. Well, actually, *I* drank the champagne. Leary about mixing alcohol with all the drugs she'd been taking, *she* drank the melted ice cubes from the bucket! After soaking in our private Jacuzzi (that is, until the complimentary bath oil caused her to break out in a rash), she began to realize that she wasn't being much fun and certainly not doing *her* part to fan the flames of my desire. So, after she toweled off, she decided it was time to slip into the special little something she'd brought along. Granted, the air conditioner was blasting cold air and she was feeling chilled, but I have to tell you—a bulky, hooded sweatshirt over a black lace nightgown does *not* do much to get a guy aroused!

Taking full advantage of my wife's guilt over practically blowing our weekend, I was *more* than willing to take her up on her offer to blow *me* instead! I stretched out on the bed, opened my robe, and closed my eyes. By now, I figured the *less* I saw, the *more* chance I had of actually getting an erection! Since she said she couldn't taste a thing, I wondered if this *one* time there might be a chance that she'd actually let me cum in her mouth. So I asked—and she agreed! With high hopes and a hard cock, I was finally close to getting what I'd come for! That's when—all of a sudden—with her mouth still around my dick, she sneezed so hard she damn near blew my balls off . . . not to mention, the thick green wad that flew out of her nose and wound up in my pubic hair!!!

106

As my apologetic wife reached for a handful of tissues and began to clean up the mess around my now limp dick, I lay there feeling completely defeated. "Oh, well," I thought to myself, "for what this room costs, I'm glad at least *one* of us shot our load!"

# FALLING HEAD OVER HEELS
*Sheri, 45*

For my husband's fiftieth birthday I decided to deal with his ongoing midlife crisis head on. In other words, I would become the sexy siren in his midlife fantasies—the pouty-lipped bombshell from one of those Victoria's Secret's catalogues. Even though I still had a body I could work with, I have to admit that after spending my days running interference between three kids, all under 10, my usual bedroom demeanor was anything *but* seductive! As a special birthday surprise for my husband, I was willing to somehow turn the look of sheer *exhaustion* into the look of sheer *eroticism*—even if only for one night!

I made arrangements several weeks in advance for my parents to babysit the kids, and secretly booked a room for the night in an out-of-the-way motel. I pored through tons of on-line selections from the Victoria's Secret's collection, and finally ordered a crimson teddy. Though I'd never be caught dead in *either,* I went to the mall for fishnets and spike heels. For a while, I wavered at the counter of a wig salon, until the saleswoman convinced me honey blonde was definitely my color (I'm a natural mousy brown). Once again, I pulled out the plastic and walked away with heaps of blond hair sitting on a Styrofoam head. By now, I felt that the one sitting on top of my shoulders needed some serious examining!

Still very uncertain that I could pull this off, I knew I needed a dress rehearsal. The very next time I was alone in the house, I dug my alter ego out of the closet. Once in costume, I stood in front of my full-length mirror, unable to decide if I looked utterly *desirable* or utterly *deranged!* Either way, I knew I needed to get my moves down pat if I had any hope at all of seducing my husband. My practice session ranged from simply trying to walk in spike heels without falling over, to choreographing a whole striptease number. After several runthroughs, all I can say is that practice *does not* necessarily make perfect, but it *did* make for some rather noticeable improvement! By the end of my private rehearsal, I actually believed I could make this a night we'd *both* remember! As I packed up my outfit for my big debut, I realized that now I was actually looking forward to strutting my stuff. For the first time in too many years I actually experienced the faint tingle of feeling sexy again!

Fast forward to the weekend of my husband's birthday. When I told him that my folks were taking the kids, his eyes lit up. When I gave him the name and address of the motel he was to meet me at, at eight sharp, his smile broadened into a shitass grin! On the way over to the motel he picked up a bottle of champagne and, when he arrived, his surprise was already there—waiting in his room! There, stretched out across the bed in all her perfumed trampiness, was his fantasy lover for the night. He just stood there in the dimly lit room, completely dumbfounded but *obviously* pleased! With soft jazz playing in the background, I invited him to come closer and make a birthday wish. When he got to the bed, I pulled him down on top of me for just a taste of what (and *who*) was to cum! I didn't stop to ask what he thought of my little surprise—his instant erection was all the encouragement I needed!

Now, in complete control (and actually enjoying the role), I pushed him down into the chair and asked him if he was ready for his birthday lap dance. Before he could answer, I started grinding my body against his to the music and I felt his penis get even stiffer. When the song ended I backed away, and although he

pleaded to let him fuck me right then, there was no way I was letting my little striptease number go to waste. Assuring him he could have it soon, I went into my dance, with each sultry maneuver revealing just a little bit more. By the time I was almost out of my teddy, I had *him* almost out of his mind! That's when, just a few moves shy of baring all, the strap of my teddy somehow got caught on the heel of my shoe. Unable to regain my balance, I tripped and fell over, twisting my ankle badly and spraining both wrists! Instead of going down *on* my husband, I wound up going down *in front of* him, and the only chance the poor man got to 'come', was to my rescue! Of little consolation was the fact that, just as the saleswoman had guaranteed, my sexy blonde wig remained perfectly in place!

# CHAPTER 8

# GIRLS JUST WANNA HAVE FUN

## THE PRICE NICE GIRLS PAY FOR BEING NAUGHTY

## GETTING NAILED
### Erica, 33

My boyfriend and I both *really* get turned on by watching each other masturbate. It's been a big part of our foreplay for years now. I'll lie back on our bed, open my legs real wide, and stroke myself while he sits opposite me in a chair so that he can jerk himself off. When we feel ourselves close to cumming, we finish each other off by fucking each other's brains out.

One time, I was really into it. I wet myself with my own saliva, and then started off deliberately slow at first, as if to tease myself into wanting more. Soon I was panting and rubbing my clit feverishly with one hand while thrusting my fingers in and out with the other. Between watching me and pulling on himself, my boyfriend had gotten as hard as a rock. Seeing his huge erection just inches away, I began pleading and grinding my hips into the mattress. He was *more* than ready to mount me and shoved his cock in as deep as it would go. We were both so close that it only took a few deep strokes for both of us to explode!

While we were cooling down and getting ready to go at it again, he reached for my hand and brought it to his mouth for a taste of my juices. Usually, all it takes is a few licks of my deliciously sticky fingers and he's ready to go all over again. His tongue was playing between my fingers when he realized that the false nail on my third finger was gone. We tried not to assume the worst, and immediately began combing every inch of the crumpled bedsheets, hoping we were wrong. No such luck. We were now *convinced* that the nail was buried deep inside my vagina . . . thanks largely to his penetration. Panic-stricken, I groped around inside with my longest finger until I thought I felt something. After try-

ing to relax in a tub of hot water for hours in hopes of being able to ease the nail out, I finally gave up and made an emergency appointment with my gynecologist. All I can say is, thank God my doctor's a woman! She didn't say a word, she just went in there, pulled it out with a pair of tweezers, held it up to the light and said, "Hey, nice color—who does your nails?"

# TOO MUCH OF A GOOD THING
## Charlotte, 29

Back when I was a sweet, innocent thing of 16, I was invited to spend a summer abroad in the home of some close family friends. Up to that point, their 18-year-old son and I had always thought of each other like brother and sister, since we'd known each other virtually all our lives. Obviously, we'd both changed a lot since he and his family moved to Europe and, as soon as I stepped off the plane, it was love at first sight for both of us! Somewhat awkward about these new feelings, we decided to keep our budding romance secret from his parents! Wanting to be alone as much as possible, we figured they'd be less apt to chaperone us everywhere we went if they didn't know we suddenly had the hots for each other! Don't forget, I was the innocent little daughter of his parents' best friends, and protecting my honor while I was in their home was uppermost in their minds. Little did they suspect that the *real* danger was right under their roof—and noses!

Since this was the first time I was away from home—not to mention, madly in love—I was hellbent on acquiring a sexual education as well as the cultural one my parents sent me over there for. As it turned out, James was as innocent as I was and had as much to learn as I did. After stealing kisses and rub-ups for weeks, I devised a new plan. His parents went to bed early and, apparently, slept like logs. When I told James that I would sneak into his room each night after his folks retired, he was aghast! Fearing that we'd get caught and that his father would kill him, he said *no way!* But, when I announced that I had no intention of giving myself to a man who wasn't willing to lay down his life for a piece of

my precious virgin pussy, he suddenly found himself caught between his cock and a hard place, and quickly agreed to risk life and limb!

So, night after night, we'd go to our separate bedrooms and listen for the sound of his parents turning in. When the coast was clear I'd slip out of *my* room, tiptoe past *their* room and run straight into my Romeo's waiting arms. Each night, for hours and hours, we'd explore the unfolding mysteries of each other's body. Each morning, before dawn, I'd scurry back to my room and drift off to sleep dreaming of my love! As the summer progressed, this became our routine. By day we kept up our platonic charade and by night I kept up his more-than-attentive cock!

Considering my total lack of previous experience, I'd actually gotten pretty good at sucking him off, but I hadn't yet tried to *deep throat* him—taking the whole thing completely in my mouth. The night before I was scheduled to fly home, I was determined to try and take my place among the ranks of the proud, sexually powerful women of the world! I attempted to take as much of his seven-inch dick into my mouth as I could. I was already on the verge of choking and, as soon as the tip hit the back of my throat, I gagged, pulled back, and vomited all over his stomach! Amazingly, he seemed much less appalled by my flawed effort than I was and, while he graciously cleaned himself off and changed the sheets, I sat in a corner—totally traumatized! So much for the song, "I Am Woman, Hear Me Roar." My new version was, "I Am Woman, Watch Me Puke!"

## THE FLAMING QUEEN
### Fernanda, Age Undisclosed

In the early days when I was embarking on my transition from Fernando to Fernanda, femme fatale, mixed in there with some of my finest hours were some rather distinctly hairy moments!

Not long after I had become "one of the gals," I was introduced to a very sweet man at a well-known transgender club downtown. Because of where we met, I didn't have much explaining to do. He was obviously familiar with the scene, and completely aware of what he was getting himself into, so to speak! Despite the fact that I still had a hose tucked into my hose, he fancied me quite the lady, which really helped pad my self-confidence to the fullness of my already padded Wonderbra! Not one to *drag* my less-than-dainty stocking feet, soon after our very proper first date I was ready to try something a bit more up close and personal. I suggested that the next time we share a romantic evening at my place and, much to my delight, he accepted without the slightest hesitation.

I agonized for days over what to wear. Tell me—what girl *ever* has *anything* in her closet? At the height of my anxiety, I made several frantic phone calls to my hair stylist, pleading with him to have my new and very expensive wig ready in time for my big night. I'd scrimped and saved for months to buy this long, flowing mane and thought of it as the *pièce de résistance* of my feminine charms. I picked it up the day before my date and was tickled pink with the honey-blonde new me!

I spent half the day making myself up, and the other half making myself

117

*For one long, agonizing moment I was torn between saving my dignity and saving my life!*

absolutely crazy! As the bewitching hour drew closer, I remembered something a more experienced lady friend had once told me: Until the hormone injections really kicked in, *candles* (not *diamonds*) were a girl's best friend! Admittedly, I might have gone overboard here because by the time my gentleman caller had arrived, several dozen fragranced candles glowed from virtually every surface of the room!

The sweetheart brought me the most exquisite bouquet of flowers, which I immediately arranged in a vase, then joined him on the couch for a drink. After some lovely chitchat and a few glasses of wine, it didn't take long before the sparks started to fly. We began with some rather pleasurable kisses, and then gradually slid ourselves down and across the length of the cushions. As he began to explore more and more of my "feminine mystique," I laid my head back on the arm of the couch. Since I was still unaccustomed to the length of my new hair, I had no idea how dangerously close the ends were to the candles burning on the side table! With no advance notice, half my wig caught fire and, for one long, agonizing moment I was torn between saving my dignity and saving my life!

When I first purchased the wig and envisioned tossing my fabulous thick head of hair around, I definitely did *not* imagine it would mean *tearing* it off my head, *flinging* it across the room, and *dousing* it with a vase full of water!

119

# FINGER-LICKIN' GOOD
## Juanita, 45

Much to my own amazement, I guess I've evolved into a fairly typical 40-something lesbian . . . the job, the lover, the house, the cats. Even though I'm settled down in a long-term monogamous relationship (going on 16 years), I *do* have my share of some pretty hot sexual experiences to look back on from my wild and crazy youth. Of course, mixed in there were some pretty embarrassing bloopers as well. I guess if I had to choose, this one qualifies as one of the funniest, though I certainly didn't think so at the time.

I'd been introduced by a mutual friend to a really hot bi-curious female. Against my better judgment, I became immediately obsessed with her. We'd been out alone casually a few times and hadn't slept together . . . *yet!* This was definitely going to be the night. I could just feel it! I slyly suggested dinner at a neighborhood steak house, "coincidentally" just a few short blocks from her apartment. Quite intentionally, I ordered a rack of juicy baby back ribs, just dripping in thick mesquite barbeque sauce. Sucking a rib down to the bone can be very suggestive if you do it right.

Anyway, I must have been putting on a really good show because, barely halfway through the meal, she gave me one of the most mouthwatering looks I'd ever gotten in my life and suggested we take a doggie bag with the rest of the dinner back to her place. I tried to look cool and only *slightly* interested but, inside, I was grinning like a Cheshire cat. I never paid a check so fast in my life!

Throwing caution to the wind, we started making out in the elevator of her building. By the time we got to her floor, we could hardly keep our hands off each other. Despite my intention not to rush things (this being her first time with a woman), as soon as the apartment door slammed behind us, I began tearing her clothes off. Before I knew it, we were rolling around on her living room floor while my tongue engaged hers in the most titillating of play. All I can say is that whatever she lacked in *experience,* she more than made up for in *enthusiasm!* Totally caught up in the heat of the moment, with nothing but green lights coming from her all the way, I started fingering the hell out of her dripping-wet cunt. If her moans and grinding hips were any indication, my hand was obviously working magic between her legs. Convinced that I could make this the most memorable night of her life, I picked up the pace, eager to get her off for the *first* of what I knew would be *many* times.

There I was, reveling in all the glory of my butch prowess when, all of a sudden, she pulled back, screamed for me to stop, and yanked my hand from between her legs! I didn't know what the hell was going on—I just backed off, totally confused. The only thing I could think of was that she just freaked out at the idea of having sex with another woman. Without saying another word, she jumped up, ran into the bathroom, and slammed the door behind her. For the next few minutes, the only thing I heard was running water. Pissed off with myself, I began picking up my clothes and swearing off bi-curious chicks for life! That's when I heard uncontrollable laughter coming from the bathroom. Now, I was *totally* confused. Still laughing, she finally came out, but, seeing the look on my face and the clothes in my hands, she rushed to explain. Apparently, the residue of barbeque sauce that remained on my fingers had gradually begun to cause a burning sensation on her swollen flesh. The deeper I went and the harder I rubbed, the more excruciating it became. Despite how

close she was to cumming, she *had* to make me stop.

I was never so relieved. On the one hand (pardon the pun), I felt terrible about her pain but, on the other, I was glad it wasn't me. After we *both* had a good laugh, she scrubbed my hands and made me finish what I'd started!

# ARMED AND DANGEROUS
## Patty, 25

Men aren't the only ones who enjoy a rowdy bachelor party at a strip club! We brides-to-be have our wild sides too and are quite capable of letting our veils down. So, naturally, I was not at all disappointed when my friends announced that they were holding my bachelorette party at Chippendales. They said that, before any walk down the aisle, a girl should experience at least one runway full of hot, magnificent men! Though it was a first for me—a few of my friends were regulars, and managed to get us the best seats in the house, literally within arm's length of the stage. I was amazed how much they knew about each of the dancers and their routines. They were like sports fanatics who'd memorized all the stats of their favorite players. They generously tried to share as much background information as they could, while consuming an equally generous amount of alcohol!

By the time the lights dimmed and the music cranked up, I was more than a little tipsy, and more than a little ready for the show to begin! Obviously, the rest of the women in the audience shared my enthusiasm, because from the very first pelvic thrust the crowd went wild! One amazing hunk after another bumped and ground his way into the secret fantasy of every woman in the room. There was the cowboy, and the construction worker, the patrolman, the pirate, the mechanic, the Marine, and the motorcycle guy. Each more gorgeous than the last, they paraded in front us with every eye color, hair texture, and skin tone guaranteed to cause a collective estrogen meltdown!

Then, just when I thought my overstimulated senses could take no more, I

123

*As he danced us off the runway and behind the curtain, everyone stood up and gave us a rousing hand.*

came face to face with the crotch of my dreams! Inspired by the frenzy of the moment (not to mention my five drinks), I rose to my rather wobbly feet and began waving a $20 bill in his direction. Because I was so drunk, it took a great effort on his part to coordinate his dance moves with my wavering hand in order for me to stuff his well-deserved tip where it belonged! After several unsuccessful attempts, we finally made contact and I shoved the bill as deep into his jockstrap as the law would allow. When he winked and threw me a kiss, I felt like we really connected—never expecting our 'connection' to turn so publicly humiliating!

Don't ask me *how*, but due to the one-in-a-million odds that have always characterized my life, my charm bracelet hooked itself to his jockstrap, making it impossible to pull my hand away! Despite our predicament, he stayed a lot calmer than I did, making every effort to free himself without missing a single (musical) beat! I, on the other hand, began to panic! In my desperation, all I could think of was to yank harder. Much to my horror, the only thing *that* did was to pull his jock strap away from his crotch! By now, *everyone* (even my so-called friends) was chanting, "Take it off! Take it off!" There must be a law prohibiting full-frontal nudity in these clubs because, instead of risking his career, he pulled me up onstage with him and finished his dance number with my bracelet and my arm hanging from his gyrating crotch! As he danced us off the runway and behind the curtain, everyone stood up and gave us a rousing hand. Unfortunately, it was *mine* that *singlehandedly* brought down the house!

Once offstage and out of the spotlight, I was able to calm down, undo the clasp, and remove the bracelet so that he could more easily unhook himself from the menacing charm. Ironically it was a miniature Statue of Liberty—a souvenir

125

from my first trip to New York City, when I was just a young girl. Somehow, I *don't* think the inscription about welcoming "your huddled masses yearning to breathe free" was *ever* meant to include the 'mass' between a Chippendales dancer's legs!

**CHAPTER 9**

# PROPS AND FLOPS

*SATISFACTION (AND PROBLEMS) GUARANTEED*

# THAT SINKING FEELING
*Sharon, 38*

I've never, *ever* admitted this to *anyone* . . . at the risk of renewing my sense of horror just thinking about it, here's the worst sexual blooper of my life!

First, let me say that I'm a successful 38-year-old stockbroker, divorced, no kids, with a pretty robust sexual appetite. Since I'm very particular about who I date, let alone sleep with, I'm often left to entertain myself with my nine-inch-rubber dildo that I've nicknamed Manny (for obvious reasons). Over the years, Manny has proved to be one of the *best* investments this stockbroker has ever made!

Anyway, one morning I woke from a dream feeling especially horny. Since I didn't have to be in the office until noon, I figured, what the hell. So, out came Manny from deep inside my dresser drawer and, as usual, I got off in no time flat. As was routine, once I finished I brought the dildo into the bathroom to rinse off before tucking it safely away until the next time. Just as I was about to turn on the faucet, the phone rang. I was going to let the answering machine get it, but it turned out to be an important rescheduling call that I couldn't afford to miss. I left Manny in the sink and raced to answer the phone. A few minutes into the conversation, the doorbell rang. With cordless in hand I walked to the front door and, through the peephole, I recognized the cute exterminator here for a routine maintenance spraying. I threw on some clothes and let him in, reminding him to pay particular attention to the areas behind the kitchen and bathroom sinks. Then, without giving it another thought, I went back to my phone conversation while the exterminator—already familiar with the layout of my apartment—went about his spraying.

129

*My heart was pounding in my chest! My face had to have been beet red!*

It wasn't until he was actually standing in the bathroom that I suddenly remembered the dildo in the sink! I became immediately weak-kneed and abruptly ended the phone conversation. I didn't know *what* to do next. I was panic-stricken and lightheaded from anxiety. For a moment I wasn't sure if I was actually going to faint! I racked my brain—what could I *possibly* do or say to justify what he had seen? I listened for his laughter, but heard nothing. After what felt like a lifetime of me pacing up and down the hall with my head in my hands, he came out of the bathroom. My heart was pounding. My face had to have been beet red. He, on the other hand, was amazingly nonchalant about the whole thing. His face was expressionless and without saying a word, he just walked past me with his can of pesticides in hand. I was stunned. Maybe he *hadn't* seen it after all. It wasn't until he was halfway out the front door that he turned and winked. "It's okay," he said, with the smuggest smile on his face, "my four-year-old daughter never puts *her* toys away after she plays with them either."

# OF HUMAN BONDAGE
## Bailey, 32

After lots of newly married conventional sex, I encouraged my wife to explore her sexual fantasies. After a degree of awkward reluctance, she finally admitted that the fantasy of being tied down and forced to have sex really turned her on. That was all I needed to hear, since the idea of bondage had long been a turn-on for me as well. I immediately went on-line and ordered every kind of physical restraint available, including harnesses, handcuffs, and leather straps. At the local hardware store, I purchased several kinds of ropes and even some bungee cords. It wasn't long before we had quite a substantial collection (including dozens of videos and numerous books and magazines on the subject) in the storage space of our headboard. There, in the private sanctum of our prim-and-proper bedroom, was our dirty little secret. It would amuse us that, within minutes, we could turn our home sweet home into a virtual S&M parlor whenever the mood struck!

A few months into our newfound hobby, my mother-in-law came to visit for the weekend. It was the first time she'd actually stayed with us, and my wife wanted to do whatever it took to make her feel welcome and at home. With this in mind, my wife insisted that she take our bedroom and that we'd sleep on the foldout sofa in the living room. In the beginning, she seemed to be having a pleasant enough time but, after the second night, I sensed a definite change in her mood and attitude toward us. I couldn't put my finger on it and asked my wife if I was just imagining things, but she acknowledged that she'd noticed it too. Not knowing if we'd inadvertently said or done anything to offend her, my

wife tried to get her mother to talk about what was bothering her. Instead of opening up, she just denied anything was wrong. We racked our brains trying to figure out what had suddenly put her so on edge. Since she wasn't talking, there wasn't much left to do but forge our way through what was left of the weekend, with everyone pretending to have a good time. All I can say is that, by the time she boarded her plane, *we* were more than ready to see her go, and *she* was more than ready to be gone!

A few days later we received the following note:

*Dear Mr. and Mrs. Houdini*

*I am happy to say that I arrived home safely and had no trouble getting a taxi from the airport. I wanted to thank you both for all your hospitality and for extending me the comfort and privacy of your bedroom. I'm sorry for any inconvenience this might have caused and even more sorry that I opened your headboard, mistakenly thinking I would find an extra blanket inside. Instead, what I got was a real education on what tying the knot means in a modernday marriage! I guess you learn something new every day, but I still prefer the old-fashioned bond I shared with your father. Call me . . . when you're not tied up with other things!*

*Love,*

*Mom*

## DO NOT DISTURB
### Wayne, 36

Being somewhat on the short end of things, I soon realized I had to go a longer way when it came to satisfying a woman than most men who were more naturally well endowed. As a result, I quickly became what one might call an expert on just about every kind of sexual paraphernalia known to heighten a woman's arousal. My arsenal of pleasure toys included an assortment of vibrators, dildos, butt plugs, *ben wa* balls, and restraints like handcuffs and ropes. Despite my so-called shortcoming, I eventually met and married a really sweet woman. She herself was on the quiet, reserved side and it took quite a while for me to break down her inhibitions about using all those things. While she certainly came to adore (and even name) each and every one of them, she would never, ever admit *her* attachment to all *our* attachments!

Anyway, for our first anniversary I splurged on a long, romantic weekend in the Big Apple. Hoping to make it even more special, I got tickets to some of the big shows, made reservations in several of the best restaurants, and booked us at the posh Plaza Hotel, right on Central Park. She couldn't have been more thrilled with my surprise! She packed *her* things, I packed *mine* and we were soon on our way with absolutely no idea just how unforgettable a trip it would be!!!

I can still recall how we both had to look away as the very polite bellhop unloaded our luggage with all the sex toys packed inside and said he hoped we enjoyed ourselves. As soon as he closed the door behind him, that's *exactly* what we did . . . in every position and with everything we brought along!

Occasionally, we'd come up for air, take in a show, eat a meal, or go for a stroll through Central Park. Having spent the first year of our marriage on a really tight budget, it was a real kick to be staying at such an exclusive hotel and being treated like royalty. After lots of late-night sex, most mornings we just stayed in bed and ordered room service. On this particular day, however, we decided to have breakfast out. Too lazy to put all our toys away, and planning to have more sex when we got back, we decided *not* to have the room made up and left everything out all over the bed. It was not until we were halfway through a relaxing breakfast in a Greenwich Village café that we realized *each* assumed the *other* had hung the Do Not Disturb sign on our door, when in fact *neither* of us had! Hoping against hope that we could make it back to our room before the maid did, we left what remained of our breakfast, hurriedly paid the bill, and hailed a cab uptown, bribing the driver with the promise of a huge tip if he drove as fast as he could. We nearly knocked the doorman down, as we raced through the lobby to the elevator bank. It felt like it took forever to get up to our floor! As soon as the doors opened, we raced out and down the hall where we saw several chambermaids congregated around their carts. It was obvious they were all whispering and laughing about something. Our stomachs twisted, knowing just what that *something* was! Like two naughty children, we slunk meekly passed them, desperately trying to avoid their eyes. We could feel them staring at us as we approached our room, opened the door, and stepped inside.

I don't think I'd ever seen my wife quite so upset as when she looked across our room. The place was immaculate—the wastebaskets were emptied, the used towels and food trays were gone, and the drapes had been opened to let in the bright morning light. She walked over to our perfectly made bed, buried her face

135

*The whole collection was arranged neatly in size places.*

in her hands, and moaned. There, leaning up against our newly fluffed pillows, were all the toys we'd left out on the bed from the night before. The whole collection was arranged neatly in size places from the largest vibrator to the smallest butt plug, with every dildo and French tickler in between! Two chocolate mints discreetly flanked the whole row! Now, *that's* what I call five-star service!

## GREAT X-PECTATIONS
### Trish, 40

You know how when two people have fantasized for a really long time about being with each other and then actually get the chance, their expectations go through the roof about how *great* and how *hot* the sex will be? Well, that's the way it was for me and a woman that I worked with. The problem was that, while we knew we both had the hots for each other, we also knew we were both in committed relationships with other people. We vowed not to act on the attraction, but the harder we tried not to think of *each other,* the harder it got to think of *anything else*! I guess it was a case of conscience *versus* cunt and, eventually, our cunts won out! So, in spite of the risk and our enormous guilt, we set an intricate plan in motion and began counting down to the big day. Needless to say, by the time we'd gotten to the appointed place and hour of our secret rendezvous, our anticipation and desire for each other was off the charts!

*She* was supplying the candles and wine to make it unforgettably romantic! *I* was supplying the vibrator and dildo to make it unforgettably raunchy! The silk negligee she'd slipped into was a complete surprise and put me totally over the edge! After all the flirting . . . after all the fantasizing . . . we were finally alone and in bed together, and I was determined to make good on my promise to make it the *best* sex she'd ever had! As things turned out, it was *memorable,* all right, but not quite in the way I had intended!

Since she'd never experienced the thrill of a vibrator, I was eager to be the first to introduce her to the exquisite sensation. After turning her on with my tongue, I reached for the cordless little wonder and held it against her clit, skillfully alternating its exact place and pressure in response to her moans. She was so wet it was hard to keep the tip from slipping off its target. Then, just as she cried out that she was about to cum, the goddamn batteries in the vibrator died and the thing stopped cold! In that moment, I finally understood how a guy must feel when *his* equipment fails him! At first she thought I was just trying to get her even hotter by keeping her on the cusp of her orgasm and for a while she played along, moaning and biting on my ear while I secretly panicked. When I tried to pick up *manually* where *it* had left off, she wasn't happy. She pulled my hand away and pleaded with me to finish her off with the vibrator. At that point I had to tell her that the Energizer Bunny was no longer "still going." It took a while for her to forgive me but, after a few more glasses of wine and a glimpse over at the dildo lying on the mattress nearby, she seemed more than willing to let me have another go at her.

For a while we just rolled around playfully on the bed, but it didn't take long before things really heated up again. She ground herself against my open palm and, no longer satisfied with the work of my fingers, she moaned for me to fuck her with "that thing." Without interrupting the rhythm of our rocking bodies, I reached out to take hold of the eight inches of rubber she wanted me to shove inside her but, much to my horror, it was no longer there! I continued to lick and tongue her, trying to buy a little more time to do a frantic sweep of the mattress with my one available arm. Unaware of my dilemma, she bucked and demanded, "Oh God! Fuck me! Fuck me with it!" I remember thinking, "Shit, this can't be happening to me! Where the hell is it? First the vibrator dies and now I can't find the goddamned dildo." Obviously, with all our moving around, it somehow got lost in the crumpled sheets and was no longer anywhere within reach! Up

139

against her impatience, I finally had no choice but to admit I had *another* problem. By now totally frustrated and fed up, she was a lot less understanding *this* time than she was the *last*. The moment was very much over, and so was any hope of the great sex I'd promised!

I convinced myself that I'd been punished for cheating, but I really don't think it should count if nobody cums. And, trust me when I say *nobody* did!

# INTERNATIONAL ARRIVALS:
# UNITED STATES OF EROTICA
*Claudia, 28*

Without apology or excuses, let me state right up front that I'm a call girl and a damn successful one at that! While I *personally* prefer the intimate companionship of another woman, my clients are all extremely wealthy *gentlemen* who are accustomed to the very best money can buy . . . *including* the best sex! So, when money is no object and infidelity is no problem, they call me! I generally will entertain a client for a few hours, either in the privacy of my duplex or at a discreet location of his choice. Occasionally, my business requires me to travel, which brings me to my little blooper.

A few years back, I had a very nice client who invited me to accompany him (for a very respectable fee) on a weeklong business trip to the French Riviera. While my nights would obviously be *his,* my days would be free to shop and bask in the Mediterranean sun. Now, *that* was an offer a working girl like me couldn't refuse! Since he lived on one coast and I on the other, the plan was for us to fly (first class, of course) from our respective cities and meet in France at the hotel. Because he'd been a regular of mine for quite some time, I knew exactly what kind of sex he liked, and took extra care to fill one entire suitcase with a wide array of S&M paraphernalia. Since he also liked to watch me masturbate while I pretended to be a parochial school student, I packed my schoolgirl uniform and my favorite vibrating dildo. I left plenty of room in my other Louis Vuitton for all the fabulous new clothes and jewelry I was *sure* he would buy me.

It was a perfectly sublime week for both of us. While *he* conducted his busi-

141

With each item she pulled out, the nuns blessed themselves over and over again!

ness affairs by day, *I* lay in the hot sun conjuring up ways to make his nights even hotter (let's just say that everything I packed was put to good use)! Judging from the extremely generous tip he added to our agreed-upon sum, I'd say he was quite satisfied and more than willing to put his money where his mouth was!

We sealed our business arrangement with a friendly kiss, parted at Charles de Gaulle airport, and boarded our separate planes back to the states. Ironically, the flight home was one of the smoothest I'd ever had. It wasn't until *after* we landed and I was on the line coming through customs that I hit some pretty wild turbulence of my own! The line was moving at a snail's pace when I took note of the three elderly nuns standing directly behind me. Bored to tears and somewhat amused by the differences in our chosen lines of work, I decided to pass the time by engaging them in some friendly conversation. Although they didn't seem to be in the habit of schmoozing with anyone wearing leopardskin tights, they told me they were returning home from a spiritual retreat and going back to their parochial-school classrooms. I was secretly amused by the irony and wondered if they knew my client as a young boy. Suddenly, in the midst of these thoughts, my vibrating dildo went off inside my luggage (I'm sure it was God's way of getting even with me for playing with three of his girls)! Naturally, the sudden buzzing raised suspicion and, in spite of the fact that I prayed for a miracle, a very large, no-nonsense female custom's agent demanded that I place my suitcase on the counter for inspection. With all three of the nuns looking curiously on, I reluctantly unlocked, unzipped, and pulled back the flap of the suitcase. There on the top was my neatly folded parochial school uniform with a huge vibrating rubber dildo stuffed into the pocket of its navy blazer! Hoping the agent had a sense of humor, I just looked her straight in the eyes and smiled

nervously. "Accessories *really* make the outfit, don't you think?" (She was *not* amused!) Meanwhile, the nuns recoiled in unison as the phallic thing continued to pulsate against the crisp white cotton hanky. The agent remained stonefaced as she removed the batteries and proceeded to go through the rather risqué contents of my suitcase. With each item she pulled out, the nuns blessed themselves over and over again. Carefully comparing my face to the photo in my passport, the agent asked me about the nature of my travel. "I guess you could call it a working vacation," I said. Apparently disgusted but aware that I was within my rights, she told me to "get this crap out of my sight and move along!" A lot less neat about it *this* time around, I collected all the stuff from the counter and quickly shoved it back into my case.

Before hurrying off, I couldn't resist turning around to the three nuns, each of whom was feverishly working her rosary beads. "What can I say girls: We *each* have our calling!"

# CHAPTER 10

# FLIRTING WITH DISASTER

DANGEROUS LIAISONS AND OTHER NEAR-FATAL ATTRACTIONS

*He kept the cowboy boots and I kept the cowgirl!*

# THE WILD, WILD WEST
### Gloria, 32

A few years back I was dating a guy who, despite the fact that a childhood pony ride was his last contact with a horse, seemed to fancy himself a real Marlboro Man. For his thirtieth birthday, I thought I'd indulge his ridiculous delusion with an expensive pair of hand-tooled cowboy boots and a surprise weekend at a dude ranch. I could never have imagined, when I made those reservations, what a surprise it would turn out to be for *me*.

Our riding instructor was an absolutely stunning redhead from Wyoming, with the deepest green eyes and most beautiful body I'd ever seen. While I kept my rather curious attraction to myself, my boyfriend was not the least bit shy about sharing his. During one of our lessons he leaned over to me and whispered, "Fuck these horses—I'd much rather be riding *her*—or, better yet, watching her ride *you!*" At first I was shocked. We'd been sleeping together for over a year and he never once brought up the idea of a threeway. Certainly the notion had never crossed *my* conservative mind . . . at least not consciously, and at least not until then! He asked how I felt about inviting her to join us later for drinks and just see where things went from there. A bit reluctant but admittedly intrigued, I rationalized that this would be his birthday bonus gift and agreed. Vicky was more than receptive and said she'd love nothing more than to spend the night with us. I didn't know how she meant that!

We agreed to meet at eight in the cocktail lounge, and immediately hit it off. As the hours wore on, I privately vacillated between being terrified and turned on by the possibility of making love with her. We were all feeling the effects of

147

our second bottle of wine when Ted finally propositioned her. Much to my amazement she didn't hesitate for a minute. On the way back to our room she whispered seductively in my ear that she couldn't wait to get between my legs and that she intended to drive me wild. Obviously, *I* was the only novice here!

Once inside the room, Ted described his birthday wish: to watch Vicky go down on me while he jerked himself off. By then, I was so nervous I couldn't say what happened next. Somehow we all wound up naked, with me lying on my back and Vicky running her exquisite tongue over every inch of my aching body. Despite my initial inhibitions, just as she predicted, she had me more turned on than I'd ever been in my life! I was so into what she was doing, I'd completely forgotten that Ted was there, that is, until he suddenly let out the most blood-curdling wail I'd ever heard. It seemed that, in an effort to get a real close look at Vicky tonguing me, he moved in only inches from the epicenter of the action and I accidentally smashed him in the nose with my knee! Vicky instinctively moved to come to his aid, but *I* couldn't have cared less! I was on the verge of the most powerful orgasm in my life and pulled her mouth back down against my clit, insisting she finish me off first. Unfortunately for him, her allegiance was with *me*. For the next few intense minutes, Ted clutched his face, moaning, "Oh no, oh no!" while I clutched the back of her head moaning, "Oh yes, oh yes!"

Later, on our way to the local emergency room, I defended my initial selfish indifference to his pain by explaining that I was just making absolutely sure that his birthday wish . . . and *I* . . . came true! Even before the bandages on his broken and reconstructed nose came off, we decided to split. He kept the cowboy boots . . . and I kept the cowgirl.

148

# CLASS OF '65—ASS OF '95
*Barry, 53*

A few years back, I found myself smack in the middle of a full-blown midlife crisis. Embarrassed as I am to admit it now, I developed all the classic signs and acted out in all the clichéd ways . . . including an affair that eventually ended an already rocky 27-year marriage.

I'd been divorced for a little over a year when I got something in the mail about my 30th high school reunion. I'd let the 20th and 25th pass without responding, since I thought the whole idea of a bunch of middle-aged fools like myself, trying to recapture a part of our long-lost youth, was not only pathetic but absurd! But now, having just leased an expensive new sports car, shed 25 pounds, and a whole lot of baggage from a bad marriage, I was *more* than ready to see how I stacked up against all my old high-school buddies.

As soon as I walked through the door, I was sorry I'd come. I was totally blown away at the toll the last 30 years had taken on everyone! If it weren't for those ridiculous "Hello, My Name Is . . ." tags on everybody's chest, I swear, I wouldn't have recognized half of them! To tell you the truth, I really found it depressing. It terrified me to be confronted with the reality of all this aging *en masse*.

I was ready to cut my losses and leave, when I spotted Julie Meyers, the girl I'd taken to our senior prom. Even from across the room, she looked every bit as gorgeous as she did that night 30 years ago! From the moment our eyes met, the same old sparks started to fly. We caught up over a few glasses of champagne, and I was secretly thrilled to learn that she was divorced and unattached as well.

As we slow-danced to all our old favorites, I could feel my depression and the years melt away. With each dance she seemed to be pressing herself harder against me. I couldn't believe how terrific it felt to be holding the homecoming queen in my arms again. I was wondering if I should bring up the past when she put her mouth to my ear and whispered, "Remember the night of our prom . . . how, afterwards, we parked in front of my house, crawled into the backseat and fucked?" Before I could respond, she licked my ear with her tongue. "How would you like to drive me home right now and fuck me the same way again?" I could feel my heart begin to race and my cock begin to stiffen! I told her my car was just a two-seater, but the backs reclined and *I* was willing if *she* was! Her hand played with *my* "stick" the whole time I was shifting the one on the car—racing like hell to get us back to her house. I pulled into her driveway, turned off the lights, and we started making out like two teenagers in heat. It amused me to see that just like in the old days, the car windows fogged up from all our heavy breathing. I don't know if she was more impressed with the *Porsche* or my *erection* but, when I lowered the plush leather seats and climbed onto her, I felt every inch the super stud I was back then!

I worked her dress up as she eagerly worked my pants down. It was obvious from the way she moved that over the years she'd picked up a thing or two about driving a guy wild. After a couple of slow deep thrusts, just to get her going, I began really pumping away. Before I knew it, she was on the verge of cumming. She was bucking and moaning, "Oh, Barry, fuck me, fuck me like you did the night of our prom!" It drove me crazy hearing her call my name and I told myself that she'd never had it that good since. Hell bent on pleasing her again, I picked up the pace and rode her even harder. That's when I felt something pop in my lower

150

back. My entire body seized up in one excruciating spasm. My history of lower-back pain immediately told me that I had just reinjured a newly healed slipped disc! I knew there was *no way* I could move . . . let alone finish the job of satisfying this incredibly hot woman. It would be at least an hour—maybe longer—before I could let her out from under me. At this point, I couldn't even raise my sorry, middle-aged ass up enough to at least get my now limp dick out of her. So, it just stayed there inside of her, shriveling up into more dead meat than she already had lying on top of her!!! Totally humiliated, I explained what had just happened and begged her to forgive me. With no hope of ever having her orgasm, she just sighed. "What do we do now?" she asked, obviously unfamiliar with this sort of injury. I felt like the biggest loser in the world. "We have to wait until the spasms subside enough for me to move. It *could* be a while." I couldn't tell if she was being sympathetic or sarcastic when she smiled and said, "Oh, well. I suppose that'll give us plenty of time to reminisce about what it was like when you were 18 and could fuck me like this *without* paralyzing yourself in the process."

## SHOWER 'HEAD' FIASCO
### Yoshi, 33

Probably having as much to do with my surroundings as with my basic nature, I lived a relatively quiet life for a gay man just on the cusp of 30.

Coming from a small, conservative Midwestern town, naturally I'd thought I'd died and gone to heaven when a few summers back I arrived—wide-eyed and bushy-tailed—in the heart of Greenwich Village to visit with my old college roommate. As it turned out, he lived in one of those glorious old prewar apartment buildings right smack on Christopher Street! The entire neighborhood was packed with cruise bars and more of the hottest-looking men than I'd ever seen in my life!

I've never been one to sleep around, especially with the whole AIDS thing but, risky or not, I swore to myself that I wasn't going back to my boring little hometown life without at least *one* torrid sexual encounter to take with me. So, one night while my friend was out of town on business, I went out cruising, determined to make my fantasy come true. As nervous as I was, I managed to pick up this incredible Adonis at one of the local leather bars and invited him back to the apartment. Judging from the massive bulge in his jeans, he was obviously "up," and more than ready for anything. When I nervously suggested that we start in the shower, he wasted no time peeling off his clothes and mine. Let's just say it was obvious he wasn't going for romance here and wasn't interested in *anything* that took all night. Despite my lack of experience with anonymous sex, I tried to remind myself that I wasn't either. I'd only been with a grand total of three men in my entire life and, except for the stack of magazines and gay porn I had in my apartment, I'd never actually *been* up close and personal with anyone that had such an incredibly hot body! To be standing there before this rock-hard god of a man left me totally dumbfounded and, for the first few blurry seconds I was absolutely sure I was in some kind of a dream . . . that is, until he turned on the shower, roughly shoved a bar of soap in my hand and commanded me to lather him up. All at once, the dream became real and I was determined to make the most of it. I did exactly as he said and knowing what he expected next, immediately dropped to my knees, eager for my taste of big-city life!

That's precisely when my dream turned into a nightmare! There I was, holding this gorgeous nine-inch cock in my mouth—feverishly devouring every delicious inch of it—when, without the *slightest* warning, scalding hot water came shooting out from the shower head and down onto my bare back and shoulders. In a sheer reflex action to the shock of the pain, I automatically clenched my teeth around the poor guy's dick, and damn near altered his life (not to mention *his* plumbing) forever! In obvious agony, and mad as hell, he grabbed his wounded cock in one hand and pushed me aside with the other. I just sat there cowering, trying to explain, while he dressed and threatened to kill me if he ever saw me on the street again. Truly afraid for my life, I stayed in the apartment for the next two days.

When my friend finally returned home from his business trip, I told him what happened and he couldn't stop laughing. He'd never thought to warn me that, in lots of older apartment buildings, it's not at all uncommon for the water pressure and temperature to change suddenly if someone else in the same line turns on their shower at the same time.

For the rest of my stay, suffice it to say that the *only* thing that got stiff after that was my neck . . . from constantly looking over my shoulder every time I dared to go out!

# THE (NOT SO) GREAT OUTDOORS
## Danny, 28

You know that warning that says, DON'T TRY THIS AT HOME, well, *this* story should come with one that says, DON'T TRY THIS OUTDOORS.

For a while, my girlfriend had been hinting around about wanting to do it outdoors, like on a blanket, somewhere private, but with maybe the *slightest* chance of being caught. Now what red-blooded American guy isn't up for starring in a lady's sexual fantasy? So, being the macho, in-control lover *I thought* I was, I told her to leave all the details to me. I drove out to the local state park, scouted out the perfect secluded spot in advance, then planned a totally romantic lunch, including a special topping for "dessert."

She was totally psyched! She even insisted we didn't have sex a week before so we'd both be *really* horny. Finally, the big day had come. I wouldn't tell her where we were going but, when we got there, she was obviously pleased with my choice. Her fantasy was about to come true. Eager to get things going, we spread the blanket out, fed each other lunch, and polished off most of the wine. We were pretty ripped, so it wasn't long before we had each other's clothes off and were rolling around on the blanket, butt naked. My girlfriend was getting pretty worked up, which told me it was time for dessert. I reached for the hidden jar of strawberry preserves and shoved my fingers way down into it. I came out with a wad of the stuff and started smearing it all across the inside of her thighs and all over her cunt. Totally surprised, she started squirming with delight and, for the moment, I couldn't have been prouder of myself for thinking of it. No sooner did I start going down on her, with the wicked intention of slowly licking every

154

bit of the sticky goo off until I had her begging to be fucked, did Mother Nature fuck *me* instead!

There she was, her legs in the air, going wild with every lick, when dozens—then hundreds—of swarming bees came out of nowhere and started diving at my head, trying to get at her crotch. How the hell was *I* supposed to know that every fucking yellow jacket within a 10-mile radius would set their hungry little stingers on the same sweet sticky bush that *I* had? We both jumped up and started waving our hands around like crazy. She was totally freaked out and screaming for me to do something. In spite of everything I tried, before she could get her panties back on she'd been stung on her cunt and thighs over a dozen times. We just grabbed our clothes and ran for the car, leaving *every-thing*—including her outdoor fantasy—behind!

All I can say is I'm glad my girlfriend isn't allergic to bee stings. Because, when I suggested that I take her to the emergency room to get checked out, she said she'd rather die from a bee sting than die from embarrassment. She spent the rest of the weekend with ice packs on her crotch and thighs and, if you don't count the back seat of a car, we haven't tried fucking outdoors since.

I recently asked her if she thought she might ever want to try doing it out-doors again. "Yeah, sure," she said, "that'll *bee* the day!"

155

# PARADISE LOST
## Connie, 28

Since practically everyone in my small hometown already knows this embarrassing story, I suppose the rest of the world might as well hear it too!

The summer between my junior and senior years of college, I took a job at a local nursery-and-garden center and immediately went ga-ga over the major hunk they'd hired to do all the really heavy hauling. He lifted weights, and had the most amazing body I'd ever seen. He knew it too, and didn't hesitate to use it to his advantage . . . in more ways than one! After watching him work bare-chested most of the day, I made sure he noticed me too and, most nights, I would go straight home and masturbate to fantasies of him fucking me. Since I was practically engaged to someone out of state, we couldn't even date, but I knew that I was *his* fantasy, too. Then, one day, we actually got the chance to turn our fantasy into a one-time-only reality. Unfortunately, the reality turned into a disaster!

One, afternoon the owner had an appointment and asked if we minded closing up for her. Not only didn't we mind, we couldn't wait! At six o'clock we practically threw the rest of the employees out, locked the door, hung the CLOSED sign, and raced to the back of the shop behind a row of huge floor-to-ceiling metal shelving units. With my fantasy about to come true, I wiggled out of my shorts and panties while he unzipped his jeans and pushed them down around his incredibly muscular thighs. The fact that he wasn't wearing any underwear and that his cock literally sprung up to meet me only excited me more. I was already soaked and panting with anticipation when he effortlessly lifted me up and set

my ass down on one of the shelves—just the right height for penetration. I moaned as he spread my legs and began playing with my breasts. He worked himself deep inside me and began slowly pumping away. With every thrust I felt myself closer and closer to cumming, totally unaware of the danger that loomed overhead. We never realized that the vibration of our slamming bodies shook the clay pots stored on the top shelf. Eventually, one fell off the edge and came crashing down on the poor guy's head. Much to my horror (and, I admit, my disappointment), he slipped out of me and fell to the ground unconscious! I was totally freaked out and couldn't tell if he was dead or alive! When I tried to wake him and he didn't move, I knew I had to call for help. Now I was *really* fucked! Hoping not to have to admit what we were doing, I quickly redressed and tried frantically to lift his torso in order to pull up *his* pants as well—but it was hopeless. He was, literally, dead weight! There was nothing left to do but call 911 and hope that *I* died before they arrived! In a lame attempt to preserve what little I could of our dignity, I yanked a leaf off the nearest plant and covered his poor, pathetic penis.

I paced, prayed, and waited—fully expecting to be charged with his murder—but, just as the ambulance and police arrived, thank God, he began to regain consciousness. Though still quite dazed and sporting a huge lump on the top of his head, it was quickly determined that his injuries weren't life threatening . . . unless you count dying of embarrassment! With everyone relieved, all the attention now shifted to the leaf covering his otherwise fully exposed groin. Unable to conceal their amusement—and assumption—the paramedics burst out laughing, while the grinning police officer took out his pad and pen and turned toward me. "Well now, Eve, it looks like you and Adam here had a little trouble

157

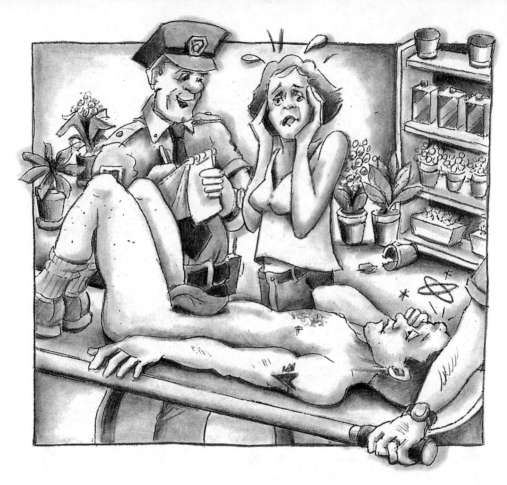

*The grinning police officer took out his pad and pen and turned toward me.*

in paradise. Why don't you fill me in on the details while he gets checked out at the hospital." I had to explain the whole humiliating story. Naturally, the owner was furious and fired us both. Even worse than losing my job, I was totally mortified when the incident—described in graphic detail—appeared in the official police blotter of our town newspaper with the headline: SINNERS EXPELLED FROM THE GARDEN OF EDEN!

I think *God* eventually forgave me. I know my *ex-fiancé* never did!

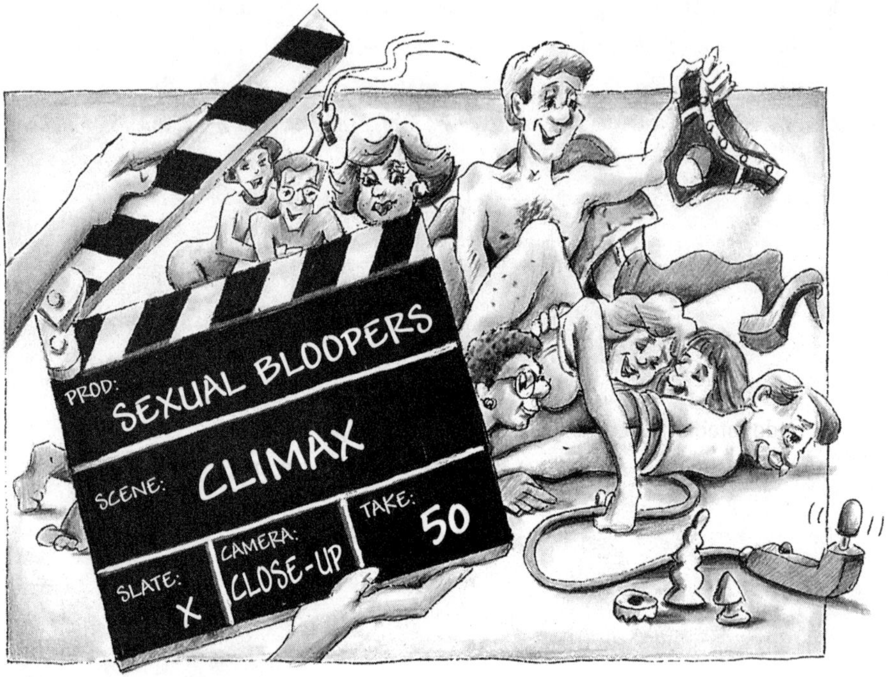
PROD:
SEXUAL BLOOPERS
SCENE:
CLIMAX
TAKE:
50
SLATE:
X
CAMERA:
CLOSE-UP

## *CLIMAX*

Now that the truth has finally been told, the next time *you* want to yell "Cut—this can't be happening to me!" you can relax knowing you're not alone! Our relentless pursuit of sexual pleasures leaves us all wide open to every kind of comic disaster imaginable. If it hasn't happened yet, it's bound to, sooner or later. As long as we remain sexual beings we will undoubtedly have our share of sexual bloopers. Why deny or secretly endure them? It's a helluva lot more fun to share and enjoy them! It's time we dismissed the myths and rejected the hype—time we ignored the expectations and chucked our collective anxiety. Forget it all! Follow your lustful libidos and revel in that rare flawless performance, because, chances are, there's a four-star blooper just waiting in the wings!

## ABOUT THE AUTHOR

For the life of her, Michelle Horwitz can't quite figure out how the heck 35 years have whizzed by since she was awarded a full scholarship to the School of Visual Arts!

As a freelance illustrator, designer, and copywriter with ties to the advertising, marketing, and giftware industries, she readily admits that nobody appreciates and harnesses the selling power of hype more than *she* does. Just the same, she confesses to having grown increasingly *weary* of it as well. A creator and licensor of new product concepts, Ms. Horwitz's specialty is social expression. *Sexual Bloopers* is her first book . . . and her idea of a little playful revenge. She's hopeful that its refreshing honesty will finally level the playing field between hype and reality where we desperately need it the most: below our collective belts and between our collective legs. She's convinced the truth will be one big, hilarious relief to our media-saturated, overstimulated psyches.

Born and raised in the boroughs of New York City, the author shares an apartment in Forest Hills, Queens, and a home in East Hampton, Long Island, with her partner Sherry Harris. They have been devoted to each other's dreams . . . and delusions . . . for the past 25 years.

These days, between all of life's major and minor distractions, Ms. Horwitz remains focused on completing her first (and sure to be bestselling) novel. Though nowhere near finished, she already knows what she'll wear to the premiere when the book is made into a major motion picture. Please don't confuse *that* with only more unrealistic hype. She just figures a little "creative visualization" can't hurt her chances!